'Nearer Than Breathing...'

Canon Melvyn Matthews is the Chancellor of Wells Cathedral in Somerset where he has responsibility for the cathedral's programme of education and spirituality. He also oversees the Ministry of Welcome to the many visitors the cathedral receives. He was for some time the Senior Chaplain to Bristol University but, before that, taught in the Department of Theology and Religious Studies in the University of Nairobi. More recently, he was the Director of the Ammerdown Centre, an ecumenical laity centre near Bath. He has written a number of books, the most recent being *Rediscovering Holiness – The Search for the Sacred Today* and *Both Alike to Thee: The Retrieval of the Mystical Way* (both published by SPCK). He is married with children and grandchildren, and enjoys sailing.

'Nearer Than Breathing...'

Biblical reflections on
God's involvement in us

Melvyn Matthews

Published in Great Britain in 2002 by
Society for Promoting Christian Knowledge
Holy Trinity Church
Marylebone Road
London NW1 4DU

WOODBROOKE
LIBRARY

231·042

The author and publisher acknowledge with thanks permission to
reproduce the following material:

Charles Causley: 'I am the Great Sun', *Collected Poems 1951–2000*,
Macmillan 2000, reprinted by permission of David Higham Associates.
Excerpt from 'The Dry Salvages', *The Four Quartets*; copyright 1941
by T. S. Eliot and renewed 1969 by Esme Valerie Eliot, reprinted by
permission of Faber and Faber Ltd, and of Harcourt Inc.
Rainer Maria Rilke: 'The Archaic Torso of Apollo', *New Poems*,
translated by Stephen Cohn, Carcanet Press Limited, 1997.
R. S. Thomas: *Counterpoint*, Bloodaxe Books, 1990.

*Every effort has been made to trace and acknowledge copyright
holders. The publisher apologizes for any errors or omissions that may
remain and, if notified, will ensure that full acknowledgements are
made in a subsequent edition of this book.*

Extracts (marked AV) from the Authorized Version of the Bible (The
King James Bible), the rights in which are vested in the Crown, are
reproduced by permission of the Crown's patentee, Cambridge
University Press.
All other biblical quotations are taken from the New Revised Standard
Version of the Bible, copyright © 1989 by the Division of Christian
Education of the National Council of the Churches of Christ in the
USA. Used by permission. All rights reserved.

British Library Cataloguing-in-Publication Data
A catalogue record for this book is available from the British Library

ISBN 0-281-05416-9

Typeset by Trinity Typing, Wark on Tweed
Printed in Great Britain by
Omnia Books Ltd, Glasgow

Contents

Preface

These little reflections on biblical themes are each short enough to be read on a train journey or last thing at night, or perhaps as a preparation for prayer, or in retreat. It is hoped that they will be of assistance to those who read them and somehow, perhaps, increase their faith in God as shown to us in the life and work of Jesus Christ. They are grouped into various themes and there is a sort of liturgical sequence to them, for they begin with the incarnation and end with the communion of saints, but there is a lot of wandering about in between. This means that the reader can move about the book at will, taking one from here or one from there, according to circumstance or mood or season. The text at the head of each chapter is normally an extract from the passage under consideration, so the scripture can be read prior to or in conjunction with the reflection.

Almost all of these reflections began as sermons and were preached in Wells Cathedral as part of my ministry there. Consequently, some of them refer to the cathedral and its architecture, for that inspires all of us who work there. I have tried to edit the text so that it reads easily but does not lose some of the immediacy, which is part of what a sermon means. Some of them were written while I was working on a book about the mystical tradition and so that reading often surfaces in what I have said, but I have tried to keep other people out of things as far as possible and speak in my own voice.

I am grateful to the regular congregation of Wells Cathedral who had to suffer these offerings in their original form, but my warmest thanks go to Wendy Dunn, secretary to the Dean and Chapter, who has done a wonderful job in reading my terrible handwriting on Monday mornings and typing up my manuscript. She is a real star. I have also been much blessed and encouraged by my wife June and by my colleagues. My grand-daughter Esmée Rebecca was baptized just as this book was finished. It is dedicated to her, with great love.

Melvyn Matthews
Wells, Feast of the Dedication of Wells Cathedral,
October 2001

Introduction

I have come to believe that the real task of the Christian preacher – and by 'preacher' I mean all those who are involved in the task of communicating the faith to others – is to enable those whom he or she addresses to see that there is something going on within them which is of God. It goes without saying that sermons and spiritual reflections addressed to others should be engaging and hopefully informative, should use imagery and argument and relate to the modern hearer's experience and all that; but unless they also somehow release an awareness that we are within the activity of God, and so possible participants in that activity, then they will have done little more than any other well-produced piece of media activity. Such a realization is not just an awareness of the existence of God but also, and more importantly, a sense of the activity of God within our existence. This will then call forth its own response and the listeners will then be able to appropriate this activity, own it for themselves, and work with it in their lives. It is not even that the sermon should convict the hearer of some sort of moral or spiritual failure and so bring repentance and renewal of life. It might well do that and there is surely a place for sermons of that kind, but what I am talking about is some sort of realization that what has been happening to the hearer can be seen in a different light. What is at stake is a form of opening of the eyes, a falling away of scales from one's sight, a discovery that, seen in a new way, what is really going on is of God. A sermon should really enable us to see things differently and, hopefully, better than we did before. A good sermon allows faith in life, as being from God, to flood the soul.

There is some theology in this. It is not just a theology of presence as far as God is concerned, but also a theology of participation, both God's active participation in what is actually happening and our responsive participation in that activity as an essential element of faith. It is a theology which happily abandons a neutrality about the processes of life, which no longer sees them as no more than the stage upon which the drama of repentance and faith is played out. The creation is not simply the setting in front of which the play is performed. Life is not that from which we must be rescued. All of what is happening is constantly God's work. What needs changing is our stance, the position from which we look, our perception, our understanding of what is. It is our feet which must shift, so that we look at things from a different place. The English theologian who was most aware of this, and who because of the prevalence of violence in her day was most in a position to turn away from such an understanding and say that this world was corrupt, was Julian of Norwich. She it is who places words in the mouth of the Trinity: 'See, I am God. See, I am in all things. See, I do all things. See, I never remove my hands from my works, nor ever shall without end. See, I guide all things to the end that I ordain them for, before time began, with the same power and wisdom and love with which I made them; how should anything be amiss?'[1]

Indeed such a way of seeing could be said to be essentially part of the tradition of English spirituality. It surfaces again in Thomas Traherne, the parish priest and mystic of the seventeenth century whose works have now begun to receive the attention they have long deserved. He repeats Julian's insight:

> The brightness and magnificence of this world, which by reason of its height and greatness is hidden from men, is Divine and Wonderful. Yet it is the cause why men understand it not. They think it too great and wide to be enjoyed. But since it is all filled with the majesty of his glory who dwelleth in it; and the goodness of the Lord filleth the world, and his wisdom shineth everywhere

within it and about it; and it aboundeth in an infinite variety of services; we need nothing but open eyes, to be ravished like the Cherubims.[2]

And the advent of postmodernism has enabled the contemporary Church to recover something of the importance of a theology of participation, such as Julian and Traherne practised before the rise of the Enlightenment.[3]

But theology is one thing and the genesis of a sermon is another. If we are to have sermons which enable those who hear them to see that there is something going on within them which is of God, then those sermons have to be generated within, or at least pass through, a similar point of awareness within the heart and mind of the preacher. Their authenticity will depend upon that. I do not think it is too much to say that sermons should come from within the preacher's own awareness of what is going on within him or her which is 'of God', and unless a sermon has actually come from (or at least gone through) this point, then it will not speak to those who listen to it except as a piece of information or moral exhortation.

I have found, in writing sermons and preparing addresses, that there comes a point in the preparation when you are forced to say to yourself, 'Do I really believe all this?' or, similarly, 'Where is all this coming from?' If it is only coming from a book, or from the preacher's need to be orthodox, or from the preacher's need to conform or impress or manipulate, or demonstrate how he has been manipulated, then the sermon will be inauthentic and a matter of unbelief or 'bad faith'. While it might well (or might well not) do the other things the preacher wants it to do – demonstrate conformity, impress or manipulate – what it will not do is bring the hearer to an awareness that God is what is going on. Quite possibly it will alienate the hearer because the words are patently the product of bad faith of some kind. What the sermon has to do is to come from a point of awareness of God in order to elicit the same awareness in those who hear.

Those with long memories might remember that we have been this way before. Harry Williams, writing in 1965, has a passage about the importance of this type of awareness. He says, 'Unless what I proposed to say came from the depths of my own experience, I was struck dumb... All I could speak of were those things which I had proved true in my own experience by living them and thus knowing them at first hand.'[4] He goes on to say that this is just how any artist sets about his work – indeed, it was how Jesus himself had set about his work and without it there would be no Christianity to talk about. What Williams found true in his own experience was resurrection, life through death, but towards the end of this section there is a sentence which, as well as being well ahead of its time, was prescient in its understanding of how to speak of the faith. He remarks how the New Testament speaks of God in sending his Holy Spirit to dwell within us, and adds, 'Must we not therefore look for God in what we are, in the whole kaleidoscope of our personal experience? And in this sense would it be wrong to speak of a Theology of the self?'

Many have followed this path since, but in the process it has become clear that while this was the right way forward, it was by no means the final word, for God could not be reduced to 'self'. Christian communication is not simply a matter of making people feel good about themselves. That is why I used the phrase earlier about enabling people to understand that 'there is something going on within them which is *of God*'. This is almost certainly what Harry Williams and those who elaborated a form of Christian existentialism at the time intended, but, to be technical for a moment, the transcendental aspects of such a faith were not sufficiently emphasized. The result was a shift towards a search for some form of authenticity, but risked an unwillingness to recognize explicitly that such authenticity could only be finally guaranteed by God. I believe that we have now come to a more healthy point in which we recognize that our task is not simply to affirm the importance of the self, but also to go on to say that what is happening to the self is the work of God. In other words we need to link what is happening to the person to the ongoing reality of God. That is what I have tried to do in these reflections.

Somewhere in the writing of Thomas Merton, the American Cistercian, there is a passage where he describes himself at work, reading. He had been allocated – or, more likely, just found – a quiet place to read in the basement of the monastery near the boiler room. He describes himself sitting there reading and 'numb with the sense of God'. I think this should, in essence, be the position of anybody who speaks to others about the mysteries of the faith. He or she should descend into the depths of themselves and into the depths of the people they are addressing and attend there to God until they are numb, and then speak, but only then. It is part of the tragedy of the Church that contemporary attempts at communication so often do not do that, but talk too much and too quickly, seeking only to persuade or tell, thus treating those who listen as if they are, literally, benighted, rather than as people who have already been given God – as all things have – but who need the catalyst of words to know that fully.

I cannot pretend that all of the reflections which this little book contains come out of such an interior silence before God as Merton speaks of. Certainly I have tried to allow that to be the case, but a busy English cathedral is not a monastery, and nor am I a monk. What I can claim is that the overwhelming theme of these reflections is the desire to allow those who will read them – as it was with those who first heard them – to discover something of that involvement of God in themselves and so to know that 'God is nearer than breathing, closer than hands and feet'.

Part One

Participating in God

~1~

'Nearer Than Breathing, Closer Than Hands and Feet'

'And the word became flesh and lived among us ...' (John 1.14)

If you go to Africa you will hear tribal legends which say that God has gone away. He was once very near, but found human company very difficult and decided to move out. The legends agree that in those early days heaven was much closer to earth than it is now – about as near as your dining-room ceiling – and this was the cause of the difficulty. Some legends say that God found the noise from downstairs intolerable; others say that the smoke from the fires and the smells from the cooking pots came up through his floorboards and he couldn't bear it; while still others say that when the women pounded their maize with their long poles, the tops of the poles knocked on his floor and disturbed his sleep. So God decided that human beings were difficult neighbours and moved out. Where he has gone is unknown. That he exists is undoubted.

And although these stories come from Africa and are very ancient, when I heard them I thought they were stories about us in the twentieth and twenty-first centuries. By and large, we too think that God has gone away. There was, perhaps, an age long ago, perhaps at the time when cathedrals were built, when God was much closer to people, but since then we have driven him away with the noise of our lives, with the smoke of our experiments and the constant knocking of our wars. Even though he was close we paid him no attention and so, in despair, he left. Where he has gone we do not know, although, as the opinion polls constantly tell us, we still believe he exists.

But, just pause for a moment. Say the legends haven't got it quite right and God didn't just 'go off' like that. Say he decided to resolve his differences with his noisy neighbours downstairs in a different way. Say he decided that all the noise and all the hustle and bustle downstairs wasn't as disagreeable as all that, but was actually interesting and attractive, indeed so interesting that he wanted to join in. So he left his upstairs and came down. But he knew that his presence would be overwhelming and might frighten little children, so he came in disguise and he is actually here, hidden away among us, watching, loving every moment, perhaps sitting out on the edges looking in, talking to all those who are on the margins, perhaps because they have found themselves excluded, but for all other purposes invisible, unable to be seen by the majority of humanity who are too busy to look for him anyway.

Or, take another scenario. Say that the legends had it entirely wrong and that God had never been in a separate room, upstairs, like one of us, but grander and more irritable. Say, in fact, he had never been there at all, but had *always* been hidden among us, always been in disguise, always been an invisible presence in and with his people, always loving, always sitting with those on the margins of the party, always trying to catch our attention. Say that was the real picture. Say he was here all of the time. Say it is us, with our sight blinded by the spurious light of civilization, who cannot see him.

Because when I read the Scriptures carefully that is the picture I find, not of an absent God who has gone away in a fury, but of a patient God who has been standing at the side of the room trying to catch my eye for a long time; but because I am so preoccupied I do not see he is there. You can see this in the Bible stories. In the beginning he was not apart, but came and talked with Adam and Eve in the garden in the cool of the evening. It was they, you may remember, who, because of their insecurity, hid from God and he had to call to them, 'Adam, where are you?' It was they who got it all wrong, who talked of anger and divine retribution and wrath, of 'he will be cross', when all God talked about was justice and mercy. 'You have talked about sacrifice,' he says, 'but I have desired justice and mercy. I have been trying to talk to you about all this but all you do is continue to address me as if I were somewhere else and as if I were different from what I am, as if I were a vengeful, absent and angry God. I've been trying to whisper to you in a still small voice, but you seem to prefer whirlwinds and tempests, violence and destruction. No wonder you crucified me in the end. Just what sort of God do you think I am?'

You see, in the end there are no barriers, no walls between us and God, no ceilings to knock on, no other place to send him. It is we who invent these things, we who place these images over the reality that God is, we who say, 'No, don't come near me, you are too kind, too loving, too much to bear.' It is we who resist or deny his loveliness.

Or it is usually. Because the story of the first Christmas is that it doesn't have to be like that. There was a point in time when some people did see that God was among them, hidden away in a stable. The people who saw this were people who had, in effect, nothing else to see. They were shepherds, socially outcast; people like Mary and Joseph, Zechariah and Elizabeth, who were not preoccupied with power, not blinded by possessions, and so could see what was really going on. To these people, the word was spoken. In these people, the word was born.

And so it continues today. God is still there, still speaking his word to us, still trying to catch our attention.

But there is one last twist to this story. Just as you are saying, 'Ah yes, perhaps you are right. Perhaps God is in disguise somewhere, perhaps I have had my eyes closed to his presence…' Just as you say that, then you might also realize that his disguise has been better than you know and that it is the person next to you that is the Messiah, that you even, I even, are the disguises which God wears. That he was born as a human being in Bethlehem is the sign that *each* human being is his word, is his face, can be his hands and feet. So when you look at another person, when you even look at yourself, it is God who looks back. When you look at a person on the margins, an African child, a poverty-stricken person, it is God who looks back, calling, 'Will you love me?' 'Will you give me your gold and frankincense and myrrh?'

He has not gone away.

He is nearer than breathing, closer than hands and feet.

~2~

The Long Lunch

'They came and saw where he was staying, and they remained with him that day. It was about four o'clock in the afternoon' (John 1.39)

One of the great advantages of the Christmas season – the blessed week or so from Christmas Day onwards – is that you can enjoy a number of long lunches. These are those occasions when over another glass of wine, or perhaps even port and cheese, you can just sit and enjoy each other's company and let the meal roll on in its own way. They are occasions when you suddenly find yourselves talking about those things which really matter and saying the things that you really mean and, in a strange way, loving each other more than you ever knew possible.

My wife and I were fortunate enough one Christmas season to share in a couple of these long, slow occasions – one with my brother and his children and their children – 15 of us altogether – and another with our great friends and their friends. On this second occasion for some reason we began talking about the human capacity to act out of guilt or compulsions from the past, 'oughts' which make demands upon us, sometimes crippling demands which can destroy. And sometimes we follow these demands rather than acting out of freedom and peace and inner grace. Although we didn't use those words it was really a conversation about redemption and forgiveness and how we are renewed – and of course there were all sorts of things in the backgrounds of each of us, some of which as friends we knew about, which coloured our conversation. It was one of those conversations where you think, 'Hang on, this is important…' and you feel you are communicating with each other at a profound level and seeing where you are. In one sense it was a glimpse of our true selves and, perhaps, a glimpse of what we wanted, truly, to be like, a sort of original blessing which sharing the meal enabled us to receive.

And I was reminded of this occasion by reading the passage from the first chapter of John's Gospel where John the Baptist and two of his disciples encounter Jesus (John 1.35–42). Of course, the passage contains all sorts of things about the identity of Jesus, about how he is greater than John the Baptist, about how he is the Messiah; but underneath and behind all that it is really a story about how a group of friends found themselves, saw their true selves suddenly, and were energized to really be, to really be who they were, beyond and above all that they ought, or thought they ought, to be – it's about their calling as people.

Essentially this passage is about a group of friends, some brothers, some cousins, being surprised, being set free in the presence of Jesus, free to realize that he was more than they had thought he was and that they too could be more than they thought. And all this happened, just as it can do for us, during a long lunch. It is during a long lunch because the text tells us; Jesus says 'Come and see' and they went and remained with him until about four in the afternoon. It was the original long lunch when, in the company of friends, eyes were opened, new possibilities glimpsed, freedom gained, and the original blessing realized and owned, and this all over against the fears and complications of life and the oughts and guilts induced by their religion.

And, of course, the way that St John's Gospel relates this first 'calling' of the disciples in this passage differs entirely from the way it is told in the first three synoptic Gospels. There the disciples are called by Jesus from their work as he walks by the Sea of Galilee, but only gradually, only slowly, do they realize that he is the Messiah. John, on the other hand, shows it all happening at once, no gradual dawning of the truth, no doubting, but all of a sudden – as if the disciples suddenly fell into a black hole, suddenly fell into a realization of grace, suddenly knew that original freedom which God gave to the creation at the beginning, and suddenly knew, with a sort of shake of the head in realization, that that is how they have to live now. They could be free, indeed quite simply, they *were* free. Why didn't they realize this before?

I believe that the immense reality of God is, after all, so close, so very close to each one of us. His immense, terrifying, freedom-giving reality actually presses in upon us at every moment, in every way, at every choice, at every relationship. He is always nearer than breathing, closer than hands and feet. What keeps us from him is not the wrong belief, as if thinking the wrong thoughts would drive him away. Nor is what keeps us from him even wrongdoing, as if our actions could drive him away – indeed he has no capacity to go away, he cannot move away from us. He is constantly driven by his own nature to be as near to us as he can, unable, unwilling to move away because of what we do or what we are, simply because he not only wants us, but actually needs us, needs us to turn and notice and respond and to suddenly let go of our own preoccupations and turn and love him. Only then is God really God, only then is he complete.

If I have not been heretical enough already I would want to say that sin, human evil, is not a question of sinful acts, doing wrong things, as if the correction to that was choosing or willing to do the right things. God is not some Calvinist headmaster with a list of rules for proper conduct. 'Sin', evil in the world, derives from 'not noticing', being preoccupied, not listening to the sounds of God next to you, breathing quietly along next to you asking, 'Do you love me?' It is when we refuse to see or hear that he is there pressing upon us, around every corner, that we begin to construct the world and our own actions in it as if there were nothing else but our own choices. Philosophically that is known as voluntarism – and a very bleak and empty view of things it is – the belief that you reach God by getting it all right. It is based on a view of human nature which sees the distance between us and God as infinite – he is far away; when in actual fact he is only as far away as our refusal to turn our heads and see him there. And it's long lunches, among other things, which enable us to see that.

There is a lovely passage in the novel *The Color Purple* by Alice Walker which illustrates this. The central character, Celie, is someone who has suffered from abuse and cannot believe in her own worth. She meets another woman, deeply liberated, a singer called 'Shug' Avery.

Celie is aghast at her:

> You telling me God love you, and you ain't never done nothing for him? I mean, not go to church, sing in the choir, feed the preacher and all like that?

But if God love me, Celie, I don't have to do all that. Unless I want to… Listen, God love everything you love – and a mess of stuff you don't. But more than anything else, God love admiration.

You saying God vain? I ast.

Naw, she say. Not vain, just wanting to share a good thing. I think it pisses God off if you walk by the color purple in a field somewhere and don't notice it.

What it do when it pissed off? I ast.

Oh, it make something else…[1]

And from that conversation begins the redemption of Celie, moving from anger and despair and so estrangement and the sins that come from that condition, into noticing, being caught by the beauty and freedom of God that is everywhere pressing upon us, saying come on, stop being angry, look over here, see what I've made for *you*.

When we attend the Eucharist, we are at a long lunch. The purpose of this meal is to get us out of ourselves and to attend to God, who constantly presses his love upon us, offering us himself, all the time. We hear words from the past, but in them he is calling; we hear the broken, hesitant words of the preacher, and in them he is calling. In the end he offers us bread, and says, 'Didn't you notice? I am here, eat me.' And the reason why we came to church for this long lunch, and dress differently, and listen carefully and move slowly, is because he is, as he is at every moment of every day, present, calling, and we do not want to miss what he is saying.

And what he says is quite simple. He says, turn your head, fall into a black hole, let me catch you.

3

The English Patient

'Do not let your hearts be troubled. Believe in God, believe also in me' (John 14.1)

Do you remember the film *The English Patient*? This was a strikingly beautiful film about someone with horrific burns who is stranded in a deserted monastery in Italy during the war. The patient and his nurse and the two or three people who come into the story are all people with troubled hearts, people who want to open their hearts but somehow are afraid, who know that somehow their hearts are unable to function properly. There is a terrible languor or sadness over all of them and the empty monastery with its dusty books and deserted rooms symbolizes the emptiness of all their hearts.

The nurse in the story – Hana – is someone who feels that whoever she loves will die. She loved her friend but she was blown up. She loves her patient, but has to administer enough morphine for him to die peaceably. She is somebody about whom it is said, 'Everyone she touches dies…' She is a parable of what we fear we are – people whose hearts are empty. In one sense Hana is right, our hearts are dusty and empty – we do create death. This is the modern condition. What we love we kill, what we hold we destroy. Our hearts are right to be troubled because they do not function properly, they are dusty and derelict. This is our condition in spite of all our technological and economic success.

When you open your heart you take a risk, you don't know where you are going. In some ways opening your heart is like stepping into an abyss, stepping off the end of yourself into an emptiness, even a darkness. Opening your heart is like opening the door into a room with no walls, a room without a floor, a room where once you are in and you have closed the door there is no way out – it is a place where you feel entirely at risk, troubled perhaps, or unquiet. 'Can I trust my heart?' is a perennial question for each one of us – if only because we fear that to do so will lead us into danger, or into silliness.

But the reason our hearts are troubled is because we have *not* trusted them. They malfunction because we haven't opened them, haven't believed what they actually contain. We have not seen what is in their depths. We have only seen their dusty surface and closed them up again.

There is, perhaps, an explanation for this. All of us, I believe, are driven by desire. The engine of the human personality is the engine of desire – it is enormously powerful, it drives us without us knowing. It drives us so hard that we answer to it even when we think we are doing something else. Desire is the engine of our heart. Desire makes us. It makes us because it points us ahead, points us into the future, points us into what we can become. And we become what we desire: architects, writers, scientists, great poets, novelists, great lovers, joyful caring friends, parents, worshippers of God. But desire also unmakes us, it unmakes us because it makes us think of what we have not got. It unmakes us because it drives us to believe that we have not got what we need, that others have what we want or need, and so we compare, we compete, we rage against those who have. Desire unmakes us because we turn ourselves into beings who define themselves over against others, so that I come into existence over against others. 'Me' is the 'me' against the rest. So we pour our energies into erecting and maintaining an independent autonomous self-created self – a 'me' of my own making. The object of my desire is then to maintain that self, and who I really am is totally unmade rather than made.

Our reading of the Gospels should lead us in a totally different direction. It should lead us to believe that this unmaking is not necessary. What Jesus does in the Gospels is to talk to people, to tease out of them by story and by example the realization that they do not need to protect themselves. Effectively he tells them that to live that way is to live with a pseudo-self, a false identity, a self of their making rather than the one they have been given by God. They have to learn to lose the self they have made for themselves in competition with others – they actually do not need it. And that is what he is saying, time and time again. He says it to the Pharisees who have cocooned themselves inside structures of religion which refuse to give life. He says it to sick people who are caught within a web of illness from which they believe they cannot escape. He says it to all those who have defined their own captivity and then locked themselves within it. What he says is what he said to Lazarus, 'Come out'. What he says is what he said to the dumb, 'Be opened'. What he said to all those who would hear was 'Open your heart'.

We must live life as gift, not as our construction. What Jesus is saying is that the desire out of which you are made is a gift in you, but it is not yours. It is God's desire for himself in you, it is God's longing for God given to you. And this desire cannot be kept captive, it cannot be owned by you, you have to let it out, let it pour out freely into your life and into the world. You have to open your heart.

We cannot quench this love, we cannot punish it, put it away and control it as if it were bad, only letting it out at office parties or on New Year's Eve. We should glory in it, allow it, release it; for this desire is ultimately not ours, not ours to own, it is God's. It is given us by God because it is the desire in us which reaches out for him. The object of our desire, ultimately, is God. The paradox is that we will never enjoy ourselves, never enjoy the world until we allow that desire in us to reach out to God. When we do that and let go, then everything else is restored to us. As Thomas Traherne says: 'You never enjoy the world aright, till the sea itself floweth in your veins, till you are clothed with the heavens, and crowned with the stars: and perceive yourself to be the sole heir of the whole world, and more than so, because men are in it who are every one sole heirs as well as you. Till you can sing and rejoice and delight in God as misers do in gold, and kings in sceptres, you never enjoy the world.'[1]

Our tragedy and the cause of all our woes is that we do not want life as a gift. We want to be able to do it all ourselves, we want to be able to prove ourselves to be mature by conquering the hidden secret gods whom we believe have the secret fire we have not got. We suspect and ultimately refuse the Christ who says, 'Look, I give you life.' What we will not do is open our hearts and step into the deep and dazzling darkness of God.

St Teresa of Avila speaks of the heart when she describes it as 'the deepest centre of the soul'. She says this must be where God himself dwells. 'The Lord appears in the centre of the soul … just as he appeared to the Apostles without entering through the door when he said to them, "Pax vobis" "Peace be with you".'[2] Each one of our hearts is that Upper Room where the risen Christ came and stood among his disciples and breathed upon them, giving them life. We have a choice. We can either believe that these hearts of ours are ours to lock, and we can live in them with the doors locked for fear of whatever enemies we imagine we have. Or we can make that room ready for the coming of God.

'Do not let your hearts be troubled. Believe in God, believe also in me…'

4

How Many Muscles in the Head of a Caterpillar?

'A sower went out to sow his seed...' (Luke 8.5)

Just imagine for a moment that as God was about to create the universe, he stopped and had second thoughts and said, no, *you* do it. And instead of him doing the creating, you had to do it – assuming that by some miracle you had already been created. What would you do? Where would you start? Would you go for the business-like approach and, after widespread consultation, come up with a five-year construction programme? Or perhaps, would you spend some time wondering whether man or woman was to be created first? But however you went about it, I suspect you wouldn't get very far. I think that after a year or so I might have created an atom or two. With some careful thought I might have made one of them positive and the other negative and made them circle each other. Doing that alone would have taken another year. Would I have actually got a great deal further? Would I have thought of protons and neutrons or anti-matter and black holes and negative gravity? Would I have had the energy to create a caterpillar? Did you know that in the head of a caterpillar there are 228 separate and distinct muscles? And we haven't even begun to think about their feet. And what about whales and their capacity for singing? Apparently whale song can be heard by other whales thousands of miles away, and different groups of whales create different 'songs' which change week after week. Or what about migration in birds or the capacity of salmon to return to their birthplace?

The more you look at the created order, the more you become aware of its deep complexity, almost its strangeness. And then it changes. The universe is in constant development, changing, moving on. Whatever the theologians have told you, the creation is not something that was done once and then finished. It is still happening and will go on happening. There are more species of living things which have come into existence and then died out than there are species of living things on the earth now. We are only a sort of snapshot, a blink in the evolutionary process, a moment in the whole story of the outpouring of creation.

These sorts of statements can cause theological panic. What about creation then? What happens to the view that God created things in six days and then stopped? Perhaps we can see how God goes about it by looking at ourselves. Just reflect for a moment on the moments of your existence when you were creative – perhaps playing an instrument, or acting in a play. What happens then? What happens is that you pour yourself out, you spend time, energy, commitment, learning, practising, preparing, and at the end you are exhausted but something has been said. And it is not just performing in a concert or acting in a play, it is life. Our job, our life's work, is a form of performance, an outpouring of energy which writes itself into the fabric of the universe. Teachers write themselves into their pupils, clergy write themselves into their congregations, parents write themselves into their children. Too often we think of ourselves as somehow over and above the process, able to observe what is going on; but actually in order to be we have to pour ourselves out, we have to write ourselves into each other, we have to sow ourselves into the universe. God's being is constituted by pouring himself out and we are his outpouring.

That is why the parable of the sower is so central and so important a part of the Christian gospel. It is a parable which occurs in all three synoptic Gospels, and whereas much of the time it is interpreted as a parable about the message of Jesus and the response of people to it, in reality it is a parable about God and his constant outpouring of himself. It is about how he constantly sows himself, throws himself about, lets himself out into the universe.

This is actually what you see when you look at the universe. It is a riot, literally a riot. It is a glorious outpouring or sowing of exuberance. Some theologians have spent a great deal of time trying to stop people from seeing the universe in this way. They have tried to persuade people that God was a watchmaker who had made something once and wound it up and left it. Instead they should have been helping them to see that he was a profligate sower, chucking seeds all over the place. The old static view has to go. One of our contemporary theologians says, in answer to the theological panic that these views cause:

> We have lost a knowable world. We have lost a servile science and an all-powerful deity. In exchange all I am offering you is a wild immeasurability … I am certain that accepting all of this randomness and unknowability gives us more, if we dare to receive it, than it takes away. I believe that what we have gained is complexity, freedom and loveliness. We have gained a universe so extraordinary that it should stun us into awe, and a God so creative that we can have confidence in such a creator's ability to sort out tiny little problems like the resurrection of the body without too much trouble …[1]

Seeing God as the profligate sower, pouring seed into the creation constantly as if there were no tomorrow has, I believe, a number of very important consequences for us. First of all, it undermines any view that we may have had about the purpose of creation. In answer to the question 'Why did God create the universe?' we have to say that he did not create the universe *for* anything at all. Certainly he did *not* create the universe *for* us as if we were sitting on the sidelines waiting for him to dish up a universe which was ours to consume, like some sort of massive Christmas dinner. No, God made, God makes the universe, and us included, for the same reason that any creative act happens, it is in itself joy, beauty, delight, fun, creativity – it is in itself an act of love.

Second, we ourselves are part of that act of love and in order to be human we too have to participate in that same profligate creativity. If we are to be really as we are made to be, then we too must be over-generous sowers of seed, pourers-out of love. That is what makes us human. In the past it has been said that what distinguishes us from the animal creation is our reason – not a bit of it, animals reason. What distinguishes us is our capacity to refuse to be what we are meant to be. We can, unlike the rest of creation, refuse to enter into the creative and redeeming processes of God, to refuse to live faithfully as sowers and keep our seed in our own baskets.

Third, each one of us is creative because creativity knows no limits. It is not just a question of painting or writing or music, it is also a question of cooking or gardening or listening or being silently attentive, or helping somebody to walk, or taking an old person to the toilet. All of this writes God's seeds into the universe in some way or another. It is the enemy which says, 'I can do nothing' – first, because it is not I who does anything anyway, but God in me; second, because such a statement is a refusal of love.

But, lastly, if you are a profligate sower then you too, just as God was, will be crucified. Your seed will fall on stony ground and will die. But that's all right, because 'unless a grain of wheat falls into the earth and dies, it remains just a single grain; but if it dies, it bears much fruit' (John 12.24). And even so there are plenty more where that one came from, immeasurable quantities, 'A good measure, pressed down, shaken together, running over, will be put into your lap' (Luke 6.38).

5

Are We Erotic Enough?

'Let him kiss me with the kisses of his mouth...' (Song of Solomon 1.2)

Occasionally you begin to realize just how important foreign travel is to people. I was talking to my brother recently, who is just coming up to retirement, and asked him what he was going to do when he stopped work. 'Oh,' he said, 'I want to travel', and this from someone who has spent the large part of his life travelling and working in East Africa. Travel, we are told, is one of the biggest world industries. Going somewhere else, whether warm or cold, is something which few modern people can resist. You could say that it is one of the great preoccupations of the Western world.

It is a reminder that what drives people, what is at the root of humanity, is something very akin to desire, or longing, a yearning which must be constantly answered, a reaching out which cannot be quenched. And in our own day foreign travel has become the focus for that reaching out, that desire – foreign travel is the mechanism we in the twentieth and twenty-first centuries have found for answering that desire. This is how we respond to what drives us. There is a yearning which must be constantly answered.

The Greeks, of course, had a word for it. They called it *Eros* – desire or yearning for the object of our desire – the word from which we derive the word *erotic*. That you will know, but it might well come as more of a surprise to you to learn that for the early Fathers – the theologians of the early Church – God was Eros, not just the source of Eros, not just its creator, but the embodiment of Eros. He it was who longed and yearned, he it was who constantly desired, he it was who constantly travelled outside of himself, who reached out of himself in ecstasy to create and to re-create – to speak his word in creation. As one of these early theologians says: 'And we may be so bold as to claim ... that the cause of all things loves all things in the superabundance of his goodness, that because of his goodness he makes all things, brings all things to perfection, holds all things together, returns all things. The divine longing (Eros) is good seeking good for the sake of the good ...'[1]

For these thinkers who guided the Church during its formative years, God is a yearning, wanting, and this way of talking about God was in fact the primary way of talking about God right up to the end of the sixteenth century. And this was the primary reason why, for those 1,600 years, the most commented upon book of the Bible in Christian circles was not one of the Gospels, not even St John's Gospel, which is the one that comes nearest to speaking of God as Eros, but the Song of Solomon – that wonderful Old Testament love poem where the woman and the man seek each other in the darkness:

> My beloved spake, and said unto me
> Rise up, my love, my fair one, and come away.
> For lo, the winter is past ...
> My beloved is mine and I am his ...
> Let him kiss me with the kisses of his mouth:
> for thy love is better than wine ...[2]

This was the text, the words which spoke of the love of God for the soul, the yearning, outgoing, travelling love for the soul, and the love of the soul for God. For what God is – Eros – that also God has made us, because he has made us in his image. And when we allow our desire to desire God, then God is at work in what he has made. Julian of Norwich stood clearly in this great tradition when she said that God was the ground of her beseeching: '… so truly there is in God a quality of thirst and longing and the power of this longing in Christ enables us to respond to his longing, and without this no soul comes to heaven. And this quality of longing and thirst comes from God's everlasting goodness …'[3]

Well, by now I can hear some of you saying, yes, that's all very well, but is this really right? What about agape – simple *doing* love – doing good deeds in a disinterested way, isn't that the true New Testament word for love – isn't Eros really a Greek concept which the New Testament turned away from? But the point is that the New Testament, perhaps without using the actual word, illustrates the Eros, the desire in God, at every step of the way. Take the parables of the lost coin and the lost sheep in Luke – do they not illustrate the longing and wanting of God until that which is lost is found? And is not the longing of the Father for the Son in the story of the Prodigal, and the joyful erotic return of the son, just what we are talking about? While we should not despise simple 'doing' love, that simple agape we have been taught about, is it not a risk that we will end up without passion – exercising a disinterested love? As Paul Tillich says, 'If the eros quality of love with respect to God is rejected, the consequence of this rejection is that love towards God becomes an impossible concept … replaced by mere obedience to God.'[4] Or, to put it more succinctly, Eros can and does include agape but not the other way around.

And just to be controversial for a moment I believe that it is just this that we suffer from in the Church – we are not erotic enough – what I mean is that we do not see Christian disciple-ship as a passion – we see it too much as a duty. Becoming and being a Christian is a falling into love, it is a wanting of God because God has placed his wanting in *you*. It is a prodigality and a sharing in that prodigality. The risk is that this prodi-gality will be wasted in a far country on dissolute living, but in the end, when we recognize what possesses us, we will redirect this passion to the Father who gave us our prodigality in the first place. As Jesus recognizes in the case of Mary Magdalene, better to have loved much than not to have loved at all.

Three consequences:

The first is to do with God. If God is Eros then he not only wants us, he needs us – he needs us to complete his love. 'How can God need us?' we say. 'How can God need anything? He is God; but no, because he is wanting, we have been created to supply his wants by wanting in return. And I actually think it is a great consolation to realize that God needs us …'

The second is to do with the erotic. We live in a culture which is obsessed with the erotic – part of the reason for this is because we have shunned it, the Church has feared and despised it. Consequently it is rampant – rootless and rudderless, nothing to do with God because all those Christians are busy doing agape, self-righteous acts – and so the secular world becomes possessed of an aimless eroticism and the Church becomes ever more puritan and censorious. Now is the time to re-sacralize the erotic and to embody our love. Our sexuality, our eroticism, the lovers' desire for each other, is an instance, a tiny glimpse of the power that drives the world.

And the third is to do with creation. Scientists are discovering that the universe is a crazy outpouring, layer upon layer of different realities. New forms replacing old forms – a veritable riot of black holes, neutrons, whale song, butterfly migration, and I know not what. It is the certain product of erotic love, of an excess of wanting. Eros enables us to discover this newly revealed creation – hidden behind the so-called natural laws which are rapidly disappearing as scientific discovery goes on apace. The new science reveals the old Eros, the true God we have politely hidden away for so long, afraid that the Christians might be shocked.

This God, this erotic God, is much ruder, much more clam-
ouring, much more desiring than the intellectual God we've
believed in before with his little agapes and self-righteous
behaviour – this one will expect more of us but also carry
us through more. She might even love us enough to carry us
through death.

~6~

How Far Does Your Personality Go?

'If you keep my commandments, you will abide in my love'
(John 15.9)

Let me begin by asking a question – just how far do you go?
How far does your personality go? Do you go as far as your
skin? Or do you not reach that far? Perhaps you feel you live
not just well within your skin, but well within your body,
never ever reaching your legs and arms, staying, in fact, 'well
within yourself'. Or perhaps, on the other hand, you are
aware that your personality regularly reaches outside of your
body, beyond your skin. How far does it go? As far as you can
reach? As far as you can spit? There are some people whose
personalities are really very large, people that you bump into
long before their bodies arrive, people whom you know are
coming long before you see them.

All this might be a bit of a caricature, but it is often the way
we think of ourselves. We think of ourselves as personality
balloons, balloons of different colours, different shapes and
sizes. These are often different in shape and size to our bodies,

but the real world is composed of all these different balloons rushing about and bumping into one another. They might all have different shapes and colours, but they have very clearly defined edges or skins, and ultimately they are all totally independent one of another. Humanity, we think, is like a bunch of balloons.

I actually think that this way of seeing ourselves has permeated very deeply into our consciousness over the last 200 years. We have come to think that this is the natural state of humanity, that we are naturally isolated individuals and that unity is 'the result of a long and bitter struggle to overcome our natural divisions'. You can hear that phrase in so many places, but I would want to affirm precisely the opposite, namely, that our natural and proper condition is unity and that we naturally and properly have been made to live in unity. Disunity is the result of a struggle against or a resistance to this natural and proper condition. Disunity is a disobedience, a mishearing or a misapprehension of how we really are and have been given to be by God. How we really are is in covenant with each other. That is the good news. There is no conflict, there is no basic war between us, there is no basic division between peoples and nations. That is the truly radical affirmation of the Christian gospel. It is radical because it cuts to the root of our illusion that what characterizes human beings is conflict. That is the great twentieth- and twenty-first-century lie.

If you look at the Gospels you will, I hope, see something of what I mean. What Jesus is doing is not teaching people that this or that is true. He is not imparting certain truths, rather he is, by teaching and then by example, trying to bring his followers to a point of realization that what they had learned, what society or their religious community had wound around them as true, was actually not true. He asserts that humanity, the world, all things live not by the law of social constructs but because of grace. God's givenness was the source of all things.

To discover this breaks the chains of oppression, breaks open new possibilities for ways of doing things.

Jesus himself lives constantly within the givenness of God and those who follow him discover that this is also possible for them and so become unlocked, not caught in the ancient web of conflict but free to be and to be for others. They discover by following him that 'others' and 'they' are not in a perpetual state of conflict. When Jesus faces any sick person, or when he faces a rejected person, or when he faces a society which insists on rejecting and crucifying him, he is saying in effect, 'It doesn't have to be like this.' You can live otherwise, you can live in grace and freedom, without limits, not as people perpetually bound to the laws of conflict and death. And so he goes to his death, and enables us to go to our deaths, in the knowledge that grace, unity and freedom rule, not conflict, not constant bloody sacrifice.

What Jesus tells us, I think, is that human beings are essentially *participative* beings – that we are made when we participate in each other and in God. If you like, we are essentially *covenanted* beings, covenanted – promised – to each other. We are unmade when we insist on our own individuality. And, to take the argument a step further, this is precisely why we find belief in God the Trinity so difficult, because we start with the idea of three persons, meaning three different personalities, three different balloons. This is a total mistake and it comes as no surprise to discover people find it difficult to believe how these three can be one. If you start with the idea of 'promised' or covenanted identity you will get much further. Each 'person' of the Trinity is only a person when it is in relationship. God's being is not being until it is in relationship, until it participates in relationship.

The same is true for ourselves – we only are when we relate. We only become when we are visited. We only live when others live with us and in us. We are essentially covenanted beings and when we see this and accept it, then good news, salvation, has come to our house and we can live in joy and in true community with each other.

Let me illustrate this from a contemporary novel. You may know Iris Murdoch's novel *The Time of the Angels*.[1] This novel is set in a rectory in south London where the rector, Carel, spends most of his time in a darkened study and has instructed his housekeeper to turn away all visitors. There are, of course, as you would expect in an Iris Murdoch novel, a number of other unusual characters living in the rectory – there is Carel's daughter, her invalid cousin and a Russian emigré and his son. All of these characters are deeply alienated, and in the course of the novel discover that the person who is the subject of their fixated attention has his or her attention fixed on somebody else. They are all isolated, picking up relationships, especially sexual ones, like chocolates out of a box. It is, perhaps, a symbol of how we are now. But also in the house, exercising a strange, but haunting influence, is an icon – an icon that nobody really looks at. It was brought to the house by the Russian emigré and is a copy of that famous icon by Rublev called 'The Hospitality of Abraham', or conveniently, 'The Trinity', where the three visitors to Abraham sit in perfect balance and equilibrium sustained by their loving attention to each other. They live in relationship. This acts as a comment upon, a critique of, how those dysfunctional human beings are in that vicarage. It says we are called to mutual trust and mutual participation in each other – but we resist. We do not believe it. We cannot trust that the universe is made by and sustained by grace and so we resist and are locked into mutual violence. 'The divine Trinity rules out all egotism – whether individual or collective – all life destroying separation, any subordination or levelling of persons. It invites all humanity to make this world a permanent eucharist of life, a feast of life. Created in God's image humanity is called to live in the image of the divine life and to share its daily bread together.'[2]

Unless we believe that, the future will be as full of bloody conflict as the past.

~7~

'Music Heard So Deeply…'

'Where were you when… the morning stars sang together…?'
(Job 38.4, 7)

I have just finished reading the most beautiful novel about a group of musicians. They play together in a quartet, a string quartet called the Maggiore, and the story is about one of them, the second violin, and his love for another musician – a pianist – who is beginning to go deaf. The story is moving and passionate, but one of the things that struck me about it was the account of how this quartet practised and the book opens with such an account. It describes their different personalities and difficulties, how the cellist is always late and flustered, and so on. But then, always before they start, they play what they call 'the Scale'. 'Every rehearsal of the Maggiore quartet begins with a very plain, very slow three octave scale on all four instruments in unison. No matter how fraught our lives have been … it reminds us that we are, when it comes to it, one. When I play this I release myself into the spirit of the quartet. I become the music …' And the story tells of the breakdown and reconstitution of the group – the loss and then the recovery of the Scale. The title of the novel, *An Equal Music*[1] is taken from a prayer by John Donne which describes heaven as 'a house where there shall be no noise, nor silence; but one equal music …'

One of the things the novel seems to be saying is that there is, at the root of things, an original music which, if you can hear and play, or rather be played by, then unity and harmony ensues. The creativity and success of the quartet depends upon the hearing of the Scale – when they fall apart, the Scale is not played, they are unable to hear it. And as I read this novel it struck me quite forcibly that such an understanding is not very far from the biblical understanding of creation. In creation God speaks his word. He speaks things into being and when his word is spoken and heard creation comes to life, order and beauty come to be; but when his word is not heard or ignored then chaos ensues. This is not just the case with the creation of the world, it also applies to the creation of good order in society. When the children of Israel listen, peace and justice flow; when they stop listening, or talk their own talk so loudly that they cannot hear the speaking of God then chaos and social disintegration follow. Life, moral order, health, salvation, beauty – all these flow from listening, from attentiveness to the original speech of God – hearing the basic scale.

You see the Christian doctrine of creation is not an attempt to answer a scientific question. It is not simply an answer to the question 'How did it all begin?' The doctrine of creation is more like an affirmation about being, it affirms that all being is from God, that my being and indeed the whole of creation, is a participation in the very being of God. To affirm the doctrine of creation is to affirm that 'God is present to me in the act of my own being, an act which proceeds directly from his will and is his gift.'[2] In other words, it is the realization that you and I and all things are spoken into being by God and remain in existence because he desires to speak, and what he wants to speak is us…, this…, everything… You have this in the Psalms. In Psalm 104, all creatures look to God for their food:

When you open your hand, they are filled with good
   things.
When you hide your face, they are dismayed …

St John's Gospel is particularly fascinating in this regard for
there the writer not only asserts that God speaks his creation
into being, but also affirms that the totality of God's speech,
what he has always been saying, is to be found in Jesus, the
pure Word of God. God speaks the fullness of his word in
Jesus Christ. He is the basic scale. He is what you have to listen
to before you can begin your own performance. And if you
read through St John's Gospel you will find this basic scale
being played, and by its speech enabling everything else to
live, to be re-formed, to stand up and be once again. Do you
remember the story about the man born blind? Jesus heals by
using the dust of the earth to make mud and puts it on the
blind man's eyes. This is a clear reference to the dust of the
earth from which Adam was made at the beginning of things.
It is an act of re-creation which deliberately recalls the first
creation. Jesus, the Word of God, has always been at work
creating and re-creating, and when Jesus, the basic scale, is
heard, then new life occurs.

But you can take this a little further. At various points in
the biblical narrative there are hints that there is a basic music,
an original scale behind everything that is. There are a number
of pointers where at a time of crisis and renewal song carries
the people forward. At the crossing of the Red Sea Moses and
the children of Israel sing 'The Lord is my strength and my
song, and he is become my salvation …' (Exodus 15.2). And
in Job, just at the final point where God answers the distress
of his servant, out of the whirlwind God says, 'Where were
you when I laid the foundations of the earth … when the
morning stars sang together?' (Job 38.4, 7). And on the cross
Jesus sings the psalms of his people. What is hinted is that at
the beginning of things and at their renewal there is song.

What are laid through the creation, like blood vessels through
a body, are lines of song, song lines which ultimately, like Jesus
the singer of God's love song, we have to take up as a refrain.
We have to hear the original song, the first scale, which is

> Music heard so deeply
> That it is not heard at all, but you are the music
> While the music lasts.[3]

Several philosophers, even psychologists and psychotherapists, have commented upon the restorative powers of music
and its capacity to reintegrate those who are disintegrated.
Some have written of the role that music plays in the treat-
ment of certain disorders such as severe facial tics and even
Parkinson's disease, disorders which 'un-music' the body.
But perhaps the most interesting is the discovery that the
architects of the great Cistercian monasteries which sprang
up across Europe in the twelfth century were aware of the
importance of music in the creation of these great buildings.
They were not just built to contain music, they were a form of
music. It is now known that these architects used a system of
acoustic jars to enhance the sonority of their buildings. They
buried large pottery vases in the vaults during construction,
often in patterns. These acoustic jars then enabled the monastery to sing more surely during the divine office. It is as if they
were constructing enormous musical instruments, great listening posts, buildings which would catch the far distant
sound of the music of God, the original scale. They were like
great acoustic saucers which would pick up and relay to a
disordered humanity the reconstructing song of the wisdom
of God. Isn't that what each of us should be?

At the end of the novel I referred to earlier, the principal
character, Michael, the second violinist, has been totally
unmade by grief at losing the woman he loves. He has left the
quartet. But he goes to a concert where she, a deaf pianist, is

playing. The music is sublime, even though deaf she hears. Michael leaves the concert in tears, but concludes that music is enough. 'Music, such music, is a sufficient gift. Why ask for happiness; why hope not to grieve? It is enough to hear such music …'

Such music is gift, grace upon grace. 'My grace is sufficient unto thee …' It is the music of God which sustains and restores and redeems whatever grief unmakes us.

Should we not play that original scale before we perform …?

~8~

'You Must Change Your Life'

'And just as Moses lifted up the serpent in the wilderness, so must the Son of Man be lifted up, that whoever believes in him may have eternal life' (John 3.14)

There is a famous poem by the German poet Rilke, entitled 'Archaic Torso of Apollo', which is about the effect upon the poet of seeing a Greek statue – or part of a statue – in the Louvre. For him this marble torso speaks, it comes to him, suffused with light.

But the bright Torso, as a lamp turned low
still shines, still sees. For how else could the hard
contour of his breast so blind you?[1]

The effect is so startling that it seems to the poet that he is not looking at the statue, but that it is looking at him. The light is such, he says,

> …There is no part of him
> that does not see you.

And then, as if that were not enough, as if you were not challenged enough already, there comes the famous last phrase, showing that this torso is not simply something to see or even be seen by, but there is a moral dimension to this seeing, and the poem concludes:

> You must change your life.

Nobody, he implies, can be in the presence of such intense beauty and get away with their life unscathed, untouched. There is a spiritual and moral demand implicit in the beauty.

I was put in mind of this poem as I was reading the conclusion of the story of Nicodemus in St John's Gospel. For this text is essentially about light and the effect of light upon us, about seeing and being seen. If you remember the story, Jesus and Nicodemus have a sort of conversation, a dialogue about being born anew. 'How can that happen?' he says, and Jesus talks about being born of the spirit. 'How can these things be?' he says, and Jesus teases him, and says, 'I thought you said you knew, you said you knew I was from God … a teacher of Israel would know these things …'

And then Nicodemus fades from the scene as Jesus talks. We can perhaps imagine Nicodemus turning away, shaking his head, slightly nonplussed – and I always feel for him, for he came in good faith, full of eagerness, thinking he was on to something, only to find he hadn't got far enough. But Jesus is unrelenting, he goes on to talk about light coming into the world and people turning away from the light because they preferred darkness.

And it was at this point that I was reminded of the poem. Perhaps Nicodemus was drawn by the light as Rilke was drawn by the beauty of the statue, but then was stopped short because he realized that the light he faced contained a moral and spiritual demand. 'You must change your life.' And it was too much. Too much was being asked and he could not meet the gaze of the Son of Man. Because that is what is happening. Nicodemus is being seen by God. He knows that and comes forward, steps out of the dark, but then becomes disturbed: 'How can this happen?' 'How can these things be?' And he cannot go on any more, cannot abide the intensity of the beauty he faces. He does not want to be seen completely and so stumbles back into the darkness. Like the poet facing the light of the torso, he recognizes that, 'There is no part of him that does not see you', but cannot change his life.

There are several things to chew on here. First is the matter of divine attraction. God is present in the world, calling all things to love him. He is present, hidden within all things as the divine lover calling to his beloved, calling to us saying, 'Arise, my love, my fair one, and come away, for now the winter is past, the rain is over and gone …'[2] God is present in and to all things, calling them, drawing them to himself, telling us how beautiful we are, telling us we have ravished his heart. This drawing power of God, this divine attraction was something known not just to the author of the Song of Solomon, but also to the earlier theologians, one of whom spoke of God as a drunken lover wandering unsteadily through creation seeking his lover. For those early Fathers the principal characteristic of God was Eros – the divine power of attraction. And in St John's Gospel it is plain that Jesus knows of this divine attraction and believes that he is part of it, for three times in the Gospel, all at crucial points, he talks about being lifted up and drawing people unto him. 'I, when I am lifted up from the earth, will draw all people to myself.' He it was who, as the face of God, had drawn Nicodemus out of the darkness and had looked at him with the gaze of love.

This way of looking at the work of God has been lost to us since the Reformation and the rise of rationalism and what historians call the Enlightenment; but now, as modernism gives way to the postmodern, there is an opportunity for the Church to return to a way of talking about God which focuses upon his attractiveness.

But ordinary people have already seen the importance of this, they already know of the power of attraction and Eros is enshrined in their consciousness. Those of you who have seen the film *American Beauty* will know what I mean. The film is a hymn to the power of Eros, and there is the most remarkable sequence where the boy next door talks of a great power of attractiveness, a benevolent power which exists behind all things. The point needs making that if Hollywood film-makers know about this divine attractiveness but the Church and Christian theologians continue to talk a totally different language, trying to convince the world that the faith is 'rational', as if that were the way to evangelize, then not only are we not keying in to contemporary consciousness, but we are also selling people short. We are not telling them who God really is, the divine lover within and beyond each human love.

But there is one more curious thing which we must chew on. It is a curious thing that in St John's Gospel – and in St John's Gospel particularly – Jesus' death on the cross is a high point. It is not a tragedy, it is a triumph; not a death, but a point of life, the point of life. It is the cross which is lifted up and is the point of attraction for all people. The reason that this is a cross is quite simply because humanity cannot bear it – it is too much and we reject the gift we are given. 'Light has come into the world and people loved darkness rather than light, because their deeds were evil' – and so the Prince of Life is killed. What we crucify is the enormous overwhelming life which pours into the world through Christ, but we turn away into darkness, we do not allow that light to change our living.

In that film *American Beauty* all of the characters are in a form of darkness. They are cut off from each other, acting out a role – the wife thinks she will be a successful saleswoman, the girl next door thinks she is a successful star. None of them can allow themselves to be ordinary and love each other. They are caught in self-deception. This is what happens in 'the world', as John calls it, and what keeps us in the wilderness and what brings judgement upon us. This is because when love appears, when the divine attraction breaks through, it requires a change, not just a change of heart, but a change of life, a conversion of manners. We have to turn and allow the gift of love to live in us. That frightens us to death because it means we have to abandon the lives we have created for ourselves – we have to abandon our 'world' and live in God's world – which we cannot imagine and cannot control. So we push it all away, and if it presses upon us too closely, too near, too demanding, then we kill it and stay as we are.

The French painter Georges Rouault began his life as a stained-glass artist. When he moved to oils he painted a whole series of the face of Christ which, with their dark lines and deep colours, could be windows. These holy faces look at you with pity and with judgement. You know they are not just a face but the pure truth facing you, facing you in love, but also with a question. Will you step out of the wilderness of this world, and of its illusions, out of its ability to make you think you are safe, will you step out into the deep and dazzling darkness of God alone? Will you face that death?

'You must change your life.'

Teaching a Stone to Talk

'I will give you words, and a wisdom ... ' (Luke 21.15)

The American writer Annie Dillard has an essay which she calls 'Teaching a Stone to Talk' in her book of the same name.[1] In it she describes a strange man she once knew who lived on an island on the west coast of America and who kept a stone on his mantelpiece. For some reason it was normally kept covered, but every morning he would uncover it and give it lessons in talking, somewhat as if it were a parrot or a child.

At first we find this very strange and are tempted to put the book away. But if we read on we are illuminated, for Annie Dillard points out that the silence of nature is our destiny. This is what we have wished upon ourselves. We have, in actual fact, decided that the creation is silent, that it is 'not holy', and we live where we want to live.

She also points out that we have been faced with the silence of the universe since our wandering in the desert at Sinai. This is the mythical origin of our present condition. For there we actually heard God speaking and found it far too loud. The record is clear, 'all the people witnessed the thunder and lightning, the sound of the trumpet, and the mountain smoking'[2] and it scared them witless. And they said to Moses, it's all right, you can speak to us, but please never let God speak to us: '... do not let God speak to us, or we will die'.

And what we have asked for that we have got. For the record shows that God agreed and sent us back to our tents and to a silence that ever since we have found unbearable. Hence the torture of the strange man who tries to make a stone talk.

But it is not just his torture – it is ours, and in our day we have come to know the difficulty that this silence of the universe presents. We have poured water over the burning bush and we cannot rekindle it. We have blown away the smoke and the fire and are wondering why all we have in our mouths is the taste of ashes. All our modernism has left us with nothing. As some contemporary theologians say, 'Secularism, speaking with a microphoned and digitally simulated voice, proclaims its own lack of values and lack of meaning. In its cyberspaces and theme parks it promotes a materialism which is soulless, aggressive, nonchalant and nihilistic …'[3] The question is how can we recover a genuine rather than a 'microphoned voice', the voice that Jesus promises in St Luke's Gospel.

But every now and again we receive a glimpse into a hidden reality, that the universe is not silent, but full of noises. I was reading the other day about the song of the whales, noises which can be heard by the whales thousands of miles away, but not by us. We learn now of the noise of the cosmos – strange radiophonic waves which can only be picked up and interpreted by expensive equipment – or the noise of stars coming into being or dying away. And then, perchance, we read Psalm 65 and find that there is a speech there after all, that the psalmists knew about it all along, that there is a speech in creation, for 'the valleys shout and sing together for joy'.

You see what we are suffering from is not so much the silence of God, but our own deafness. For reasons to do with our own purposes, our need to possess and speak with our own voices, we have in fact made ourselves deaf to the song of creation. There is a great gap between post-Enlightenment thinking about nature, a form of thinking which regards nature as neutral or dead, speechless, and consequently 'ours' to own or possess or use, and pre-Enlightenment thinking when the creation was naturally understood to be alive with the praise of God. Annie Dillard's strange man is like a witness to that earlier possibility, waiting for it to return, waiting for us and the creation to remember that, once upon a time, we could all talk, that we had a voice.

One of the central means for the recovery of this original voice is prayer. For most of us prayer is a dead language, something that we have given up as forgotten or never spoken. It's like Latin, something which people used to speak, but which we moderns don't need any more. There are, of course, some strange people, scholars or vicars and monks, who might still speak this language, but most of us have moved on and don't need it any more. Prayer is not so much a dead language, rather it is a forgotten language, it is the forgotten speech of our true selves. It's not dead so much as unused.

If you read the Fathers of the early Church you will, I think, be surprised to find there references to prayer as being the natural speech of creation. For them, the whole creation 'prays'. There are some remarkable passages which speak of this, including one from the Apostolic Tradition which encourages us to pray during the night, as monks still do:

> We have to pray at this hour because all creation rests then for a moment in order to praise the Lord. The stars, the trees, the waves stop for an instant and together with the choir of angels and the voices of the righteous, sing the praises of God.[4]

The original insight of the early Fathers is that prayer is the natural uninhibited speech of the creation, ourselves included. That prayer is what we are naturally made for. This insight actually turns on its head the modern assumption that prayer is something which you have to learn or try to learn as if it is something unnatural or essentially alien to the liberated modern person.

You see, part of the trick is realizing that prayer is not your own speech, not something which you have to do. Prayer is rather the work of the Spirit, God's speech within us. Much of the time we think that prayer is some sort of work we have to do, like mowing the lawn on a Sunday afternoon when we would rather be snoozing or reading a good book. Certainly we have to choose to pray, but prayer is much deeper than something which we do. It is an entering into the speech of the Spirit, and that speech has been planted deep within us since our making.

Two writers on prayer have called it 'primary speech' and say, 'Prayer is that primordial discourse in which we assert, however clumsily or eloquently, our own being',[5] and the earlier tradition is that prayer is a participation in the language of the Trinity, for the converse between the Father and the Son in the Spirit is the original speech which makes all things and in which our prayer participates. The people who know this best, it seems to me, are not church people nor even theologians, but poets and novelists. Seamus Heaney knows about it. In one of his essays he is commenting on a poem by another writer and says, 'The lines are inhabited by certain profoundly true tones, which, as Robert Frost put is, "were before words were, living in the cave of the mouth".'[6] So deep in each one, deep within the cave of the mouth, there is the original song, the original speech, and our task is to loose the catch on our tongues, to turn the lock and allow the praise of God to emerge. When we do that we shall be who we are meant to be – truly human beings.

So, when you worship, and there is, hopefully, a silence before or during the worship and then you open your mouth to sing, what you are doing is much more than you think. You are allowing God to do what he has always done, sing within you and the stone that you were has talked.

~10~

Believing in the Trinity

'Father, I desire that those also, whom you have given me, may be with me where I am, to see my glory, which you have given me because you loved me before the foundation of the world' (John 17.24)

When I was working in East Africa I was once asked to write about the differences between the Christian and the Islamic view of God. One of the reasons for this was that East Africa had, and still has, a very significant Muslim population and that the students I taught were both Muslim and Christian. I can remember, as I worked through this exercise, that I became more and more convinced of the importance of the similarities between the Islamic and Christian understanding of God rather than their differences. I think my Christian students were perhaps disappointed that I did not point up the differences more sharply than I did, thus enabling them to preserve their difference and distinct identity as Christians over against their Muslim friends. Because what I said was that both Christians and Muslims believed implicitly in the unity of God. Both communities were totally monotheistic, and there is a singleness and unity in God which both faiths share and which is basic and cannot in any way be diluted or diminished. Indeed, I went on to say that Christians are not very good at believing in the unity of God. We might say, if we are asked, that we are monotheists, but all the time we talk about God the Father, God the Son and God the Holy Spirit in such a way that we give the firm impression, in spite of our protestations, that we are tri-theists.

You can imagine the consternation that this caused among

my mission-educated students, consternation that their lec-
turer had implied that they were polytheists of some kind. But
before you chuckle too much, ask yourselves whether or not
such a criticism could not be levelled at the Church in this
country today. For when we talk about God the Father, God
the Son and God the Holy Spirit, three persons in one God, do
we not somehow tacitly assume three separate identities?
Three selves? Three distinct Gods? And to push the point
home further, is not the widespread rise in the churches of
devotion to Jesus, who is said by some to have died on the
cross to satisfy the wrath of his Father, only further evidence
of the way in which we separate the persons of the Trinity,
such that they individually perform different functions at the
behest of and in subordination to one another? Is not this
further evidence of our capacity to separate out the persons of
the Godhead in such a way as to erect a form of virtual tri-
theism? And this especially when it is clear from the ancient
formulations of the doctrine that there is no subordination of
one person to another in the Godhead?

Well, I may exaggerate, and I hope I do, but I think not. If we
listen to popular expressions of Christianity we will discover
that Jesus and the Father and the Holy Spirit are talked about
in separate categories, as separate persons with distinct functions. The Son redeems, the Father creates, the Spirit enlivens,
such that we cannot easily see their unity or describe their
oneness with any confidence. That has become notional. Or, if
we don't do that, we talk about God in a quite simplistic, deistic
way, talking about a God without any form except as some sort
of benevolent force at work in the universe. In either case,
whether we separate the persons of the Trinity into distinct
individuals set in a hierarchy, or whether we talk about God as
some sort of benevolent being, we evacuate the doctrine of the
Trinity of its original and primary meaning.

What I said to my students then is what I still believe. The
doctrine of the Trinity is a way, the Christian's way, of talking

about the unity of God. We are talking about the one God and we are compelled, by faithful reflection on the way the faith has been given to us, to talk about God in this particular way. We are primarily monotheists, albeit monotheists of a particular kind, and so should be able to reach out to other monotheists, other children of Abraham (as our Jewish and Islamic brothers and sisters are), in conversation about God and face an effectively polytheistic world with a common witness to the sovereignty of that one God in the babel of voices around us.

There are reasons why Christians have been drawn away from the original monotheism of Jesus. We have been seduced by this word 'person' – three *persons* in one God. Because of our nineteenth- and twentieth-century inheritance and the emphasis we in the West place upon the importance of individual separate selves, we have placed that perspective over our understanding of God and looked at the expression 'three persons' through the coloured spectacles of twentieth- and twenty-first-century individualism. Consequently the persons of the Trinity are given far more personhood than the word 'persona' originally intended. The word 'person' has come to mean something different now. But scholars of the doctrine, especially those who are involved in the quest to retrieve the doctrine for the twenty-first century, are desperately trying to find a new word to convey the old meaning – and they say such things as 'There are three relationships in God, three ways in which God expresses himself', and so on. But whatever phrase they come up with, what they mean is that there is life in God but that this is life within the unity. God's being is differentiated and is not static.

Let me provide you with an image. It is said that when Columbus was sailing happily across the Atlantic he eventually espied three islands on the horizon, but as he sailed nearer he realized that what he had seen was three mountain tops on one island. So he named the island Trinidad, Spanish for Trinity, which it remains to this day. Good story, but it has a flaw. The three mountains do not speak to each other, they do not relate. Better to imagine the relationships within God in another way. Music is one way of seeing it. When you listen to a choir sing Palestrina you will hear the different voices listening to and responding to each other. Each voice has to maintain its own line, but it also has to listen to what else is happening so that in the end a single piece of music is expressed. The great discipline of choral music is learning to sing your own line yet also listening to and responding to another line behind or next to you. That is essentially a trinitarian discipline. It models the relationships in God, and actually catches us into its music just as God does.

But another way of talking is perhaps even more telling, and that is the image of pregnancy. A pregnant mother is a unity of relationships. She is the source, within her is the baby, the embodiment of new life, but they are joined by the placenta, that living stream of life which joins the Father and the Son. In pregnancy, the mother 'goes forth from herself', becomes another to herself, but is not herself diminished in so doing. Indeed she is enhanced, and that going forth from herself is enabled and conveyed by the living placenta which enables growth and communication between the persons in one body.

All of these images are inadequate, but they help us to see how in God there is a sharing of personality and life and how these relationships enhance and enrich the unity of the Godhead. They show that what Christians are doing when they talk about the Trinity is talking about the unity that God is in such a way that Jesus is seen to be God not on his own, but because he is already in the Father and the Father in him.

But there is a sting in the tail. Jesus does not only say that he and the Father are one, but that his disciples, us, his Church, are also involved in all this. Believing in the Trinity is not merely an exercise in thinking on a Sunday morning. If we believe in the doctrine of the Trinity, then we will live in a differentiated unity as the mother and the child live together, or as the different lines of music live together in the single music of the choir. We will listen to each other and open and close our mouths in sequence, and in unity as the music requires. We will accompany each other and resource and serve and listen to each other as we sing. Our tunes will then sing more surely and, perhaps without knowing it, we shall be talking about God.

Part Two

Victims and Forgiveness

~11~

Getting out of Egypt with Lionel Blue

'I have eagerly desired to eat this Passover with you before I suffer…' (Luke 22.15)

We live in an age which creates victims as almost no other. Almost the defining characteristic of the twentieth century was its capacity to create millions upon millions of victims. The last war was one which had at its secret heart the creation of over six million Jewish victims in the Holocaust – men, women and children who were destroyed simply because they were Jewish. Our country, as others in Europe, is disfigured by racism. Jews are spat at on the tube, Muslims are lampooned in our cartoons and newspapers. Foreign refugees are murdered without cause. In Northern Ireland, Catholics and Protestants have been the mutual victims of each other's hatred for generations. We also create victims in the name of justice when really justice, in the popular mind, has come to mean revenge or reparation. Crowds stand outside courtrooms shouting for death. Our age, it seems, feeds on victims, creates them, destroys them, and then goes on for more.

All of this is profoundly opposed to the essence of Christianity – because what Jesus did in his life and death was to show us how to live without creating victims: he demonstrated that living life as it was made to be lived was to live without sacrifice, without the sacrifice of others, without victims. His death on the cross is the self-offering of the final victim, the last sacrifice.

If you look at his ministry what he was doing was calling

together a group of followers who were, he believed, the essence of Israel. They constituted what Israel should be. Israel, he implied, was in collusion with the occupying power, devoted to a form of militant apostasy, and this was a betrayal of its true vocation. His ministry was to recall Israel to its true path – and so he and his disciples were the kernel of the new way. They were the new Israel called out of Egypt, given the new law upon the mountain, given manna in the wilderness and then called to follow Jesus – the new Moses – into the new Jerusalem. This little band of pilgrims were those who realized in their fellowship what Israel had been intended to realize all along. The real return from exile, the real return of God to Zion – predicted by the prophets – was happening in and through his ministry and the restored community of disciples around him. Of course, this claim was controversial, and of course it led to his death. The temple authorities could not tolerate the challenge.

But we should not miss the essential point. The challenge of Jesus' community was because it was a totally inclusive society. It was a community where there were no outsiders, a community which included all those who were victims in the society of the time. In the society of Israel there were always scapegoats, outsiders – bleeding women, women quite simply, tax collectors, people who couldn't pay their taxes, demoniacs, shepherds, the halt, the lame, the blind; the list is endless. These sinners (and 'sinners' in much of the New Testament means those who are not wanted) were those Jesus ate with. He established table fellowship with them and led them into Jerusalem, much to everybody else's disgust. These are the prodigals – those who have gone into a far country, consorted with prostitutes, fed the pigs, betrayed their inheritance, but who through the ministry of Jesus have returned to the open arms of the ever-waiting father. This community of prodigals was one where victims were no more. Nobody was scapegoated.

As Jesus and his inclusive community move closer to his final confrontation with the authorities it becomes apparent that Jesus reaches further back into his faith for resources by which he and his friends can understand their role. He reaches right back, past the prophets, back to the beginning of Israel's existence – back to their deliverance out of Egypt and the Passover experience. As the Passover looms in Jerusalem, Jesus gathers his disciples and effectively tells them that they are the Passover community and celebrates the Passover meal with them. This is deeply significant, for in Egypt the children of Israel were victims – slaves, outsiders – and what was constituted by the Passover and the exodus and the law was a community in which victimage was no more. The Passover established a new kind of people, one which was chosen by God, drawn out of subjection and slavery into the freedom of God by his gift and grace alone. It had to be different, not because they were racially superior, but because in this community there were no victims. And all of the laws, all of the Ten Commandments, all of the feasts, are meant to reaffirm that. The Ten Commandments ensure love and respect for each other, no enslaving of others. The book Exodus repeats time and time again, remember the alien in your midst, you were once an alien; remember the sojourner, you sojourned in Egypt. This new society was to be the one based on no victimage, and the celebration of the Passover meal was a celebration of Israel as a community where the making of victims was not permissible.

But Jesus comes to celebrate this Passover with his friends with an inner realization. He celebrates the Passover knowing that the creation of victims will not end unless he accepts the death of a victim himself. So, after a great struggle, he goes to his death as the willing, innocent victim in order to demonstrate what society is doing and to be vindicated by God.

But if this is the case, if this explanation of the meaning of Jesus' ministry is anywhere near correct, just think what it means …

It means that the Church, the body of Christ's disciples, has to be in society now what Jesus' disciples were then – the Passover community, bringing out of Egypt life's victims, calling those who are the victims of our age into a new community. The Church is that community which lives so much in the freedom of God himself that it can take into itself the lame, the halt, the blind, the victims of our day. It must be the community which challenges the creation of victims by others, which refuses to point the finger, which abhors those crowds of people which gather outside courtrooms to jeer and shout at those facing a fair trial, which challenges the desire for *revenge*. The Church must also be the society which challenges our own desires to be victims, our own desire to cast ourselves into the role of the excluded one and to say, 'Yes, I have been a victim and need reparation.' For we not only create victims, but we also turn ourselves, willingly, into victims so that others may take the blame which might really be ours.

But is that what the Church is like? When I look around at the Church today we appear to be totally preoccupied with other things, causes, projects which are nothing to do with the gospel as I've outlined it. We are preoccupied with new national management structures, language about customer service, and millennial projects of one kind or another, and there is little or no talk about the inward renewal of the whole Church as a community which calls together the halt or the lame or the blind so that those who are excluded can know that the waiting Father will welcome them home. What talk is there about the spiritual shape of our communities and whether we are, unwittingly, creating victims, excluding others on the grounds of race, denomination or sexual orientation? What work are we doing to rediscover our roots as a Passover community where victims are not created, but actively called in to fellowship? Or are we just the religious shine on the spirit of the age?

When I was the director of an ecumenical conference centre we used to run a weekend for people with HIV and AIDS. It involved Anglican, Catholic and Jewish clergy bringing people from different cities to rest and reflect with each other. Some of our regular staff, to my shame, refused to work while 'those people' were there – thereby confirming the worst fears of those infected of social exclusion by so-called religious people. On the Friday night Rabbi Lionel Blue, the well-known radio personality, would conduct a Jewish Passover meal and talk about the Jews as the community set free under God, and as the community which drew victims into protective fellowship. And he would ask the assembled retreatants, some of them quite ill, to walk around the Passover table singing, 'Go down Moses, tell ol' Pharaoh, set my people free …' And they would walk around weeping as their inclusion in the Passover community was affirmed.

I believe, that at heart, that is the meaning of the Christian Eucharist. We are calling each other, all victims, into table fellowship with the waiting Father. The trouble is that many people can't stand being called to live in this way and would prefer to go back to the safety of Egypt.

~12~

'I Think You Should Unravel Yourself…'

'Let anyone among you who is without sin be the first to throw a stone at her' (John 8.7)

In my last parish I was quite friendly with the local Roman Catholic priest – he was a young Englishman with a deeply ironic sense of humour and very refreshing to have around. But I remember well the occasion when he told me that he was moving to another parish. It was a bright summer day and we were at the village fête, walking slowly around the field together. And I can remember feeling sad that he was going and then, as the conversation went on, saying something like, 'Oh, it seems that I shall be here for some years' and he said, 'Oh, I think you should stay here for a long time and unravel yourself in this place and with these people ...' 'I think you should unravel yourself ...' It was a strange thing to say but it has a relevance to the significance of Lent.

Lent is the time set aside for unravelling. We human beings are strange creatures, full, it seems, of deep complexities, complexities which stem from layers and layers of memories, laid down within us like layers and layers of rock in the earth, layers and layers of stratified memories which then solidify and become dense and heavy within us. These heavy layers of memory and history become such that they then govern who we are, they lock us into preconceptions and presuppositions, prejudices which determine our attitudes, our views of others, of the Church, of our prospects, of what is going to happen as well as what is past. We become fearful, ungenerous people because we cannot escape from the layers of memory which calcify round our hearts. We are kept captive and so keep others captive, by a sort of sclerosis of memory, a set of prejudices about things which the Bible and the Christian tradition calls hardness of heart.

This sclerosis, this hardness of heart, is evident in the incident of the woman taken in adultery in St John's Gospel (8.1–11). This story is really a story about purity and identity, the moral purity of the community and the danger of its break-up unless certain behaviour, called immoral, is checked. Looked at in this light, the woman and her behaviour is being used by the scribes and Pharisees for their own purposes; what she has done, who she is, is not really in their minds –

their own identity is what is really at stake. So the story is about the mindset of those who present this woman to Jesus. It is about the landlocked way they have of dealing, or rather not dealing, with such a situation. At one level they are setting a trap for Jesus. 'Condemn her', they are saying, 'and show you are a traditionalist, or do not condemn her and so expose yourself as a woolly liberal.' But at a deeper, less conscious level they are saying, 'We do not know how to deal with this. We are aware of the requirements of both law and mercy, but we cannot resolve the issue. We are frightened of the consequences. Our hearts are unwilling to unravel themselves.' So they throw the problem at Jesus. They project their dividedness on to him and say, 'Either condemn her or we will condemn you.' Faced with such sclerosis, such an inability to let the blood of compassion flow through their hearts, Jesus is silent.

And it is this silence which, to my mind, is the most remarkable element in the story. Jesus stoops down and writes on the ground. He indicates by this that he is not going to get caught in their identity games, their games about purity and danger which use this woman's actions, so he writes on the ground. It's almost as if he is thereby reaching into another level of existence, into a depth of life or being which is outside or beyond their ken. He is silent and reaches into God. Then, when they persist in their games, when they persist in having an answer – the truth, the certainty, the undeniable judgement – he simply looks up and asks a question about their sin, and goes on writing on the ground.

By means of that silence and that questioning Jesus reaches into the reality of God and begins the process of the unravelling of their hearts. Seamus Heaney, the poet, is also deeply struck by Jesus' silence in this story and comments that it is a sort of poetry which renews the situation from within.[1] What I think it does is unravel their hearts. Jesus reaches up and finds the loose end of the tight ball of string which is their heart, and picks it free and everything comes loose. He breaks up the calcification around their hearts and dismembers their wrath. So they go away.

And all this is in total accord with so many of Jesus' words in the Gospels – his words about the woman who had washed his feet with her hair; his words about prostitutes going into the kingdom before the scribes and Pharisees; his words about leaving the wheat and tares together for God to sort out.

But it shows several things:

It asks today's Church questions about boundaries, about purity and exclusion. We might believe that we are not racist, we might believe that we are not anti-Jewish, but there are those who still want a Church of true and pure believers whose boundaries are clear about biblical truth, about the place of women, about the place of homosexuals or whoever, and play games, like scribes and Pharisees, about purity and identity. Lent might well be an opportunity for us to ask ourselves who it is we do not want, and who it is we want, to present to Jesus for condemnation.

But the story also asks us deeply disturbing questions about our hearts. Are they willing to be unravelled? Will you allow the edifices of anxiety and security and identity to be broken down? Can Christ pull upon the string and unravel you, unravel the tight ball of fear and self-righteousness within you so that you are no longer driven to condemn others?

Lent is a time for unravelling. Sin derives from the fear of what will happen if your identity is undone. Will you allow Christ to pull at the string and unravel your heart?

13

'More Pieces Than I Began with…'

'… how often should I forgive? As many as seven times?'
(Matthew 18.21)

A little while ago there was a series of television programmes which documented the effect that being held hostage had on people. Those who were interviewed were not the well-known personalities like Terry Waite or John McCarthy, but a number of relatively unknown people who had been caught up in the terrorist incidents of the 1980s and who had been held in captivity for longer or shorter periods of time with the prospect of death always just around the corner.

You might have reasonably expected these people to have come out of their period of captivity full of resentment or anger, feeling very negative towards the group that had held them; or, perhaps, permanently damaged or traumatized in some way. Not so. The files showed that as a direct result of his imprisonment one man decided to mend his marriage; another decided to put his business on a more honest footing; another, who had been a pleasure-bound journalist, returned to the Church and went regularly on retreat – much to the puzzlement of his wife and family. The producer of the programme said that he could have repeated these stories many times over.

Reflection on all this – and on the much longer periods of incarceration endured by people like Brian Keenan in particular – leads one to believe that whereas these things should never have happened – that they were an horrific offence against humanity and served nothing politically – nevertheless they had a very profound and long-lasting effect upon those who endured them. It was almost as if they discovered themselves more, or perhaps were forced to abandon certain things about their lives which they knew they did not need or want. In religious terms these people went through a 'stripping' – what the old tradition called an ascesis. It was not just that they were deprived of food or human companionship or all of the normal things that one expects in Western society, but more than that – they somehow experienced a stripping of their personalities. They were reduced to essentials.

They had to spend some time alone with themselves, so the question of who they really were and what they wanted to become became a central question – perhaps a question which they would not have had to face otherwise. This 'stripping' down to essentials meant that they had to lead the ascetical life without really wishing it upon themselves, and so were able to discover what they really wanted – namely love and loyalty in their marriages, integrity in their lives, God even – in an involuntary manner. In the stories of the Desert Fathers, those renegade monks who chose to go into the desert rather than be sucked into an unholy alliance between Church and State, the monks were told, 'Stay in your cell and your cell will teach you everything.' What the Desert Fathers sought by choice, these hostages were given by circumstances.

Brian Keenan came out of his long and cruel and senseless incarceration and said that he felt as if he were a combination of Rip Van Winkle and Humpty Dumpty – someone who had woken from a very long sleep to find that all of his parts were before him, but (and this is the significant sentence) there were more pieces than he began with! In other words, his imprisonment had enabled him to find more of himself than he knew about. In religious terms, he had found God.

If we just pause for a moment and reflect on all this there are several things which need saying. You see, the assumptions of most of us – and this would include those who were taken captive by terrorists and who figured in those television programmes – are that Western society gives us all that we as human beings have a right to expect as what we might call 'fullness of life'. We all assume, maybe unwittingly, that 'stripping', or any sort of deprivation, is not on the agenda if we are to be full human beings; but here we are faced with people who actually became and continued to choose to become more real, more fulfilled, more of themselves, because they had undergone such a stripping. We talk glibly about fulfilment, we talk about having all we need; the society of which we are a part talks endlessly about fulfilment and people spend vast sums of money in order to achieve this nirvana. Fulfilment is offered at every turn, fulfilment in your marriage or your sex life, fulfilment in your career, fulfilment of your bank balance. Religion now has become part of this.

I was in a waiting room a while back flicking through the glossy magazines when I came across a supplement on living the good life, which involved diet and exercise and good financial planning and similar things. Over the page was the final fulfilment – going on a religious retreat. A number of retreat houses were listed where once your body was fulfilled and your insurance broker had given you good advice, you could go to add the icing on the cake with a little bit of fulfilling spirituality.

I thought that it would have to be one of those retreat houses where they never read the passage, 'He who loses his life for my sake…' (Matthew 10.39). For the Christian tradition has always maintained that a fulfilled life, a truly spiritual life, is one which accepts loss and self-denial; and that the acceptance of loss and the loving choice of self-denial are part of what the Christian readily offers to God as the road to the fulfilment opens before you. I believe that ultimately Christianity teaches that all of us are radically incomplete, and that fulfilment only comes when we accept and own and bless that incompleteness.

But there is something more. It is not just that Western

society regards the acceptance of loss or the loving embrace of self-denial with disdain, there is also the question of delusion. For those returned captives, authentic living also involved a capacity to relinquish what they felt was false about themselves and their lifestyles. We can be, and often are, in a state of delusion about ourselves. And modern life appears straightforward, appears very good, but it contains the most profound capacity for falsehood and enables people to generate other identities, ways of being which are masks, performances, ways of being which are essentially dishonest and which we are best without. Our ego-selves create these identities and we live with them in such a way that eventually we become them and even think it good to become them because that is how you 'get on', or 'get noticed', or 'become something' in today's world. Thomas Merton talks about modern life as being 'illusory', narcissistic, self-regarding. He says this illusory and narcissistic life is promoted by society so that we cease to live in the truth, cease to live before God. We become part of the chattering gossipmongers. Henri Nouwen says:

> When our life ceases to be inward and private, conversation degenerates into mere gossip. We rarely meet a man who can tell us any news which he has not read in a newspaper or been told by his neighbour; and for the most part, the only difference between us and our fellow is that he has seen the newspaper, or been out to tea, and we have not. In proportion as our inward life fails, we go more constantly and desperately to the Post Office. You may depend upon it, that the poor fellow who walks away with the greatest number of letters, proud of his extensive correspondence, has not heard from himself this long while.[1]

So there is a need for an ascesis – a stripping, a stripping of our bloated requirements and a stripping away of our illusions, in order to bring us into the truth before God. The spiritual life is then a movement, a conscious 'owned' movement of the soul which requires great courage. It is a movement from a quest for self-fulfilment to a self-abandonment, from a life of self-delusion to a life of honesty before God.

How can this be done? Well, with difficulty is the first thing to say. But once that is accepted, you can embark on a difficult journey – the journey of prayer. Prayer is not just asking, what is going on in our prayer is something much more profound than we realize. The life of prayer is an encounter with the ultimate hidden reality of God. Real prayer slowly strips away our illusions; helps us to abandon what we thought we needed; reintegrates our fragmented consciousness and enables us to see things as they really are. It is the only real way out of the illusions of the self and its supposed needs. What happens in prayer is that the false self slowly falls away and the true self, honest before God, emerges.

When that happens we come face to face with the terrible reality of God. I say terrible reality because that is what God is – a deep and dazzling darkness in the face of which all of our illusions are purged away. When we come face to face with God we will find we cannot bear the reality, for we are face to face with a total whirlwind, a whirlwind of generosity which will enable us to know the truth of the parable of the unmerciful official, to forgive our enemies seventy times seven, to remit the debts of all, even to 10,000 talents, to set the captive free and to deliver the prisoners. We won't need to ask whether we are fulfilled, the whirlwind of God will have broken us into pieces, but we will find there are more pieces than we began with...

14

Eating with Defiled Hands

*'… there is nothing outside a person that by going in can defile,
but the things that come out are what defile' (Mark 7.15)*

The story of Jesus' encounter with the Pharisees in Mark 7,
and his conversation with them about what it is that truly
defiles a person, is a dangerous one for Christians to read. It
is dangerous because it can reinforce prejudice and instil false
pride. It can reinforce prejudice because it can lead us into a
false view of Judaism as being a legalistic, pharisaic religion
concerned with food taboos and the so-called minutiae of
religious observance. It can instil false pride because it will
make us think that we are not like that, we've left all that
behind, have developed beyond all that stuff. In either case,
we would be wrong.

Let's look at the question of legalism first of all. There is no
question, in this or any other Gospel text, of Jesus speaking
against the Jewish law. There are no grounds for understanding Jesus as somebody who regarded the Jewish Torah and its
provisions as bizarre or barbaric or outmoded or 'legalistic',
whatever that means. He was not opposed to Judaism as a
religious system. He was a good observant Jew who attended
synagogue and asked others to observe the provisions of the
Torah.

What Jesus and his followers were criticizing was not the
Torah, but the use of the Torah to delineate and maintain
religious and ethnic purity as over against others who were,
supposedly, impure. What was happening at the time of Jesus
was that many Pharisees were making an explicit link between
the observance of the law and national and ethnic purity over

against others. Whereas the original laws of Leviticus and Numbers did not make any link between their observance and national identity, many Pharisees of Jesus' day did make such a nationalistic connection and Jesus was deeply opposed to this. Zeal for national purity was not the purpose of the law. Observance of the law should derive from a renewed heart, that was of first importance. The law was not a weapon with which others might be cast out of the camp. Jesus looked to the prophets – Ezekiel and Jeremiah – and reminded his hearers that God's kingdom came when a new heart was given to us, not when zeal for purity ensured the eviction of the impure from the land or from the nation.

Then there is the question of false pride. If you had thought that Christianity or the Christian Church had left behind all that legalism and was a superior sort of religion, then you only have to look around you and see. The debate has not gone away. There are still those within the Church who are desperate for some form of purity, and who will use the moral law to batter their congregations and their bishops with similar calls to so-called purity. They claim pure biblical teaching about sexual ethics, or pure teaching about male or clerical authority. In recent days we have seen faithful and long-serving church organists dismissed from their posts because they are not married to their long-standing partners; children refused baptism because their parents are 'living in sin'; couples refused marriage for the same reason; and bishops of the Church barred from their parish churches because they apparently refuse to accept pure 'biblical' morality. All of these instances are precisely what Jesus spoke against, namely, the use of the moral law to achieve communal purity over against others. Time and time again he witnessed against this and asked those who knew themselves to be without sin to cast the first stone. A short while ago the Bishop of Worcester – who has been prevented from administering confirmation in a parish in his diocese because of his alleged views on homosexuality – wrote in the *Church Times* saying that it was not part of the gospel to try to erect a 'pure' Church. What we should be doing is talking about the Church as a community of grace and forgiveness. So before we become too proud and talk about Christianity as having superseded the legalism of the Pharisees, let us look around us. Let us indeed look into our own hearts and ask ourselves what we are doing and saying in the Church today, for the argument is not over. Jesus' teaching is still needed, and you do not escape merely by saying you are a Christian and Christianity has superseded legalistic Judaism. Judaism is not legalistic in that sense and many Christians are just as pharisaical as what they presume to condemn.

The truth of the matter is that this incident in St Mark's Gospel is not about all that. It is about being given a new heart. If we go back to basics and ask ourselves what it was that Jesus was doing, we discover that Jesus was a prophet of the end-time. He said that what we hoped for at the end of time or at the end of our lives was here, now, among us. Here, hidden in our daily lives, the kingdom, the life of God, could be found. And we could, if we wanted, turn away from our preoccupations about who was right and wrong, who was pure or not. We could, to use theological language, 'repent' and believe this, and find the grace and life of God being given to us now. We could enter the kingdom now. There was a realm of grace and we could live in it. This is the whole meaning of Jesus' answer to the Pharisees when they catch him and his disciples eating corn in the field on the Sabbath (Mark 2.23–30). Jesus effectively says, the Sabbath is here. The final Sabbath of love and mercy is here among us. My disciples are living in the end-time now. And the same answer applies when he is criticized by the Pharisaic Thought Police for healing on the Sabbath. 'Ah,' he says, 'in the Sabbath of the kingdom all of us will be healed and I am living in that Sabbath now. Why,' he asks by implication, 'Why are you not doing the same? Why are you, by your rigidity, effectively excluding this poor woman from the healing love of God? Just who do you think you are?' You may remember that little dialogue from Mark 2 where we are told that John's disciples and the disciples of the Pharisees were fasting, but Jesus' disciples were not and people asked why this was. Jesus said, 'The wedding guests cannot fast while the bridegroom is with them!' In other words, there is a wedding on. The marriage feast of the kingdom is being celebrated now. Why aren't you going in? God's time has broken in, the kingdom is among you. But time and time again they show they could not do this. They turn away, they have too much they want to preserve, they somehow want to continue their search for purity. Jesus makes it clear that if they are not careful, others will enter this kingdom before them – prostitutes and sinners will go in before you, he says.

British society is one in which the mechanisms of social exclusion lie just below the surface. When we cannot bear our own confusions and difficulties, we heap them upon others and drive them out. Miroslav Wolf, the Croatian theologian, says, 'The pursuit of a false purity emerges as a central aspect of sin – the enforced purity of a person or a community that sets itself apart from the defiled world in a hypocritical sinlessness and excludes the boundary-breaking other from its heart and its world.'[1] He goes on to speculate why we do this, but the fundamental reason, I believe, is because we cannot believe that God in his generosity has spread the table of his banquet before us now and invites all of us to come in out of the cold.

I was once in Jerusalem on a study tour and on the Friday afternoon the members of the group were dispersed to Jewish homes to celebrate the arrival of the Sabbath. Three of us, three priests, one Catholic, two Anglicans of different persuasions, were allocated to a professional Jewish couple who had invited another couple to help them cope. The men took us to synagogue while the women prepared the meal. The synagogue service was wonderfully chaotic with the three Christian priests struggling to follow the psalms in Hebrew, while everybody else chatted and gossiped. When we returned to the house the meal was ready, and we were asked to wash our hands in the ritual manner that observant Jews follow. I could see Mark 7 going through each of our minds. What were we to do? Should we acquiesce in what some would call unchristian practice? Should we say, 'Oh no thank you, we Christians have grown out of all that'? Of course not. All three of us gladly washed our hands in the prescribed manner and we sat down together, male and female, Jew and Gentile, Catholic and Protestant, to welcome the Sabbath with clean hands and thankful, open hearts.

It was a parable of the gospel.

Part Three

Two Women

15

In Praise of Hildegard of Bingen – Obit 17 September 1179

If you go on a guided tour of Wells Cathedral in Somerset you will discover that it is the first cathedral in England to be built in the Gothic style. It has pointed arches and ribbed vaulting, and was completed about fifty or sixty years after its commencement in 1180. These bare architectural facts hide a deeper reality, which is that this cathedral, those that preceded it in France, and those that followed it in the next hundred years or so, are all examples of the enormous flourishing of Christian faith and life which took place in Europe in the twelfth and thirteenth centuries. This was a great flourishing which saw the growth of religious orders. St Bernard and the Cistercians were transforming the monastic life, St Francis of Assisi and St Dominic were founding the mendicant orders, and there was much else besides. The Church was becoming aware of itself as a great spiritual force.

Just one year before Wells Cathedral was begun, in 1179, there died in Germany another example of this explosion of faith and life, a person who is still, I think, little known in church circles, but who is a singular and important example of what was going on at that time. This person was not a cathedral builder, although she did commission the building of a large and influential monastery on the Rhine. She was more a builder of souls, a writer and visionary who had an extraordinary influence on the religious life and thought of her day, but who was almost totally forgotten about until recent years. She is the saint whom the Church of England now officially celebrates on 17 September each year, Hildegard of Bingen. Hildegard was an abbess who lived on the Rhine between 1098 and 1179 and who has been brought into the calendar of the Church of England as part of the recent liturgical revisions. Because she is little known and because she symbolizes so much that was important for the Church then which is also important for the renewal of our life today, it is worthwhile spending a few moments reflecting on the meaning of her life.

Put briefly, Hildegard was born of a noble family in the Rhine country and at a very young age was placed in the care of a religious community. She eventually became the abbess and eventually moved her community to Bingen, on the Rhine, where a new monastery was built for them. Hildegard had become very influential and began recording her extra-ordinary visions in the 1140s. She wrote theological treatises, medical and scientific books, and a large amount of poetry and music. She became a good friend of the Cistercians and of Bernard of Clairvaux. She influenced the Popes of the time and the German Emperor, but also, as a strong and influential woman, opposed much corruption and abuse in Church and State. She wrote fearless letters to kings and archbishops reproving them for their lack of probity. So she combined prophecy with vision. At one stage she was asked to help in the Church's dealings with the Cathars in southern France, but had no more success than anybody else. She became known as 'The Sybil of the Rhine' and, as a strong medieval woman prophet and visionary, she has been a great inspiration and support in recent years to the female struggle to win approval for the ordination of women.

In trying to understand Hildegard and her importance we have to see her in the context of the twelfth century when a number of writers and thinkers in the Church were realizing something of the centrality of Christ's incarnation in the world.

The fact that God took up humanity in the man Jesus was a sign for them of how humanity was the vehicle of God's presence. God dwells in Jesus, but because he dwelt in Jesus he also dwells in each person. What we have done is lose sight of that. We have lost sight of his image in us, but have to retrieve that and allow it to blossom and flourish in us if we are to be truly human. We have to allow God to be born in us. In many ways this is a form of religious humanism and the writers of the twelfth-century Church were Christian humanists, deeply optimistic about the capacity of human beings to bear and realize the divine life within them. The Cistercians, especially Bernard of Clairvaux and Aelred of Rievaulx, with his understanding of the importance of the divine friendship God has planted in us, were the leaders in this Christian humanism.

Hildegard is very much part of this movement. She speaks of the way in which we are bearers of God. In one of her visions she sees a human being in the centre of the world, a world which in turn is resting in the womb of God, and she says, 'You are encircled by the arms of the mystery of God.' It might surprise you, but these ideas – that the world and humanity were a form of birth from the womb of God – were quite common at this time. What Hildegard does is to enlarge this view and to give it clear maternal and feminine characteristics. Earlier theologians had insisted that men bore the image of God more clearly because of their capacity for reason, but Hildegard insists on parity and does not accept that man can bear the image of God without woman. She says, 'But the human species still needed a support that was a match for it. So God gave the first man a helper in the form of a woman, who was man's mirror image, and in her the whole human race was present in a latent way.' So in many ways it could be said that Hildegard believes that woman is at least as representative a human being as man – if not more so. She pushes beyond the normal theological views which made women subordinate because they were not rational by saying that rationality cannot flourish without being in the presence of the feminine.

But there is a second reason why Hildegard's thinking was important. In common with so many thinkers of her day Hildegard saw the creation as God's handiwork. But she pushes the metaphors further than others by talking of the 'greenness' that the Spirit of God brings to all things. The creation is filled with a lush greenness which is the power of God's Spirit. The Spirit is *veriditas*, 'greenness', and Christ is greenness incarnate. All things dry up, especially people and institutions, and the Church and those in authority, so they need the reviving Spirit of God, his sap as it were, his Spirit, to bring them back into life and into flower. In one of her poems Hildegard writes of God saying:

> I am the breeze that nurtures all things green
> I encourage blossoms to flourish with ripening fruits.
> I am the rain coming from the dew
> That causes the grasses to laugh with the joy of life.[1]

This accent on 'greenness', the sap of life which is the energy of God in all things, gives Hildegard a particular place in the history of Christian thinking. This was her specific contribution, and it was a powerful weapon in her hands as she used it to castigate bishops and Popes who had dried up before their time. There are, of course, other ideas in Hildegard's repertoire, but already you can see how she took the explosion of Christian humanism of her day and widened its boundaries even further. She was not the only woman theologian of her day. Brigitta of Sweden and our own Julian of Norwich do as much. Sadly, however, apart from the Beguines in Belgium and Holland, in the next century these emphases were then lost as the Reformation and then the Enlightenment darkened our imaginations, whatever other benefits they brought. Nor should we believe that Hildegard and her companions were feminists before their time. In many ways they remained allied to very primitive views of the place of women in the Church, but something opened up in those years even if it was not taken to its conclusions.

What can we say now?

First, we have to recognize that a theology of the importance of the feminine is not a twentieth-century invention. It formed part of the faith in the twelfth century, and was part of the great revival of faith which gave us our cathedrals.

Second, that we are still struggling to articulate and express these ideas and their consequences now and we still have a long way to go before their power and creativity is recognized as authentically part of Christian thinking. I was reading only this weekend of a new episcopal appointment, a man who was inclined to believe, it was reported, that Christianity was inherently a male-dominated faith. Obviously he does not celebrate Hildegard of Bingen each September.

Third, we still need to recover a theology in which God's word and God's Spirit express themselves in us and in creation. Neither humanity nor the rest of creation is objective or neutral as far as God is concerned. We and it are an expression of his life. We are what God says. Only such a theology will enable us to value ourselves, each other, and the world in which we live.

But lastly and most important: if we are to be true to what our cathedrals mean as we try to express their meaning and the meaning of the faith they embody in the modern world, then we must use as much imagination in our thinking and talking as those who were thinking and talking when they were built. There is plainly a challenge there for those who claim to interpret the past – for at the moment the past, especially as embodied in Hildegard, is far more imaginative and open-minded than the present.

16

Julian of Norwich

'The LORD has taken away the judgements against you'
(Zephaniah 3.15)

I was in a meeting recently with the representative of the company which produces cathedral guide books. The company representative was urging us to find one or two themes which might characterize our cathedral so that the guide book represented the essential nature of this building. 'What adjectives would you use', he asked, 'when describing this cathedral?' And we thought of the lightness of the stone and the joyous character of the carvings and the beauty and colour of the golden window above the quire and so on. As we talked I was reminded that there is nothing in this cathedral which speaks of judgement. There is no portrayal of Christ as Judge, there is no Last Judgement window, and the West Front of Wells Cathedral is a welcome rather than a judgement. Since that conversation I have looked and wondered whether my understanding was correct. Surely there must be a judgement scene here somewhere? But there is not. The nearest one gets to it is a wooden reredos in one of the chapels which is a harrowing of hell, where Christ releases the victims, but that is not a judgement. It has been said that the original windows of the Wells chapter house were of the Last Judgement, as befits the place where people were judged by the dean and chapter, but this is pure speculation and the only surviving windows there are of the resurrection.

So what is this place? What is this building which is completely devoid of any sense of judgement? What sort of cathedral is it whose iconography contains nothing about

God's condemnation of sin? Hadn't the master mason read his Bible? Had he not gone to church in Advent and heard sermons about the axe being laid at the root of the tree and the bad trees being thrown into the fire? Did he and his colleagues deliberately ignore all that? Did they ignore all that about winnowing and the burning of chaff?

Well, I don't know what they knew or what they had read, but what is clear is that the masons of Wells were not the only ones to affirm that there is no wrath in God. Some hundred and fifty years or more after this cathedral was dedicated, a woman recluse in East Anglia, whose name we do not know, but who has been called Julian because of the Church she inhabited, came to the same conclusions – that when we look at God we can see no wrath in him. There is no judgement in him, the only judgement is his love.

I was reminded of Dame Julian of Norwich during our conversation with the guide-book representative but I thought I had better check my facts. So I opened Julian's book of *Revelations* and there it was: 'I saw truly that our Lord was never angry, and never will be … God is that goodness which cannot be angry, for God is nothing but goodness. Our soul is united to him who is unchangeable goodness … and between our soul and God there is no wrath …'[1]

She doesn't say there is no sin. She doesn't say that human beings do not need repentance and forgiveness. Indeed, in the very same paragraph in which these words occur there is the explicit affirmation 'it seemed to me that it was necessary to know that we are sinners and commit many evil deeds … so that we deserve pain, blame and wrath' – but the statement still stands, that in God there is no wrath …

A little later in her book Julian tells a parable. She says she saw in her mind's eye a Lord and his servant. The Lord was sitting in state with the servant ready before him, and the Lord sends the servant away on an errand. The servant 'dashes off and runs at great speed, loving to do his Lord's will', but he is so enthusiastic he falls into a ditch and finds himself all in difficulty and apparently without any assistance. Julian says several things about the servant in the ditch.

She says that he is so preoccupied with his own condition that he cannot see his loving Lord who is very close to him.

She also says that she looked carefully to see if she could detect any fault in the servant, or if the Lord would impute to him any kind of blame, 'and truly none was seen, for the only cause of his falling was his goodwill and his great desire'.

The reason we fall out of God's sight, Julian implies, is nothing to do with God, whose gaze is constant, but to do with our preoccupation with our task. We become, she says, blinded in our reason and perplexed in our mind 'so that we had almost forgotten our own love'. So we become disordered and forget our reason for being and the true object of our lives. 'We had almost forgotten our own love' is a very telling phrase. But the fact of our preoccupation, the reality of our forgetfulness, does not alter the truth that our Lord constantly stands next to us and, as she says, 'looks on us most tenderly'.

Julian goes on to say that there is a moment of wakefulness, a moment when what she calls our 'spiritual eye' will be opened. There will be a return when we will turn and see and acknowledge our haste and preoccupation with achievement, our foolishness, and come to see that the Lord was always standing there looking at us tenderly. Indeed, a few pages later in the book she goes so far as to say that in this wakeful moment we will see not just that the Lord is standing next to us, but that he is seated within us. 'He sits there erect in the soul, in peace and rest, and he rules and guards heaven and earth and everything that is.'

And before you dismiss this, as one Anglican bishop did, as 'the fantastic tittle-tattle of a hysterical woman', it might be worth reflecting that there are a number of contemporary theologians who come to similar conclusions although their language is different. They don't talk of ditches or of running in haste, but they do talk about a form of self-preoccupation which cuts us off from the recognition of God. One of these[2] talks about our preoccupation with imitating others, our rush to be like the latest shiny person. He says we always rush to copy, and so are locked into competitive desires and so produce inevitably conflictual living. We cannot, it seems, be content with who we are, that seems to be a form of pain, and so we set off to alleviate that pain by imitation and so conflict and violence. But, he says, this does not exist in God. In God there is no rush to imitate, no conflictual violence. This life, found in Jesus, is always his parallel to our own, always, in Julian's terms, stands next to us. The moment of grace occurs when we allow ourselves to dispense with copying, when we are enabled, by the witness of the gospel story lying parallel to our conflictual society, to drop the competition and be content to be who it is that God has made us.

Up until then it is we who have to run the world, but there comes a point when we know we do not have to do that because we know that our Lord is near. 'Nearer than breathing, closer than hands and feet.' This moment of disclosure is the Advent of our peace.

Such a theology, cast in both psychological and social terms by a modern theologian, is not so very different from that of Julian of Norwich. For both, the judgement is not in God, but in us and in our condition. As Julian says, 'Only our pain blames and punishes.'

Some time ago I was being interviewed on a television programme about Wells Cathedral. It was one of those programmes which tell you what there is to see in Somerset. We were standing on the Cathedral Green on a summer's day and the interviewer said, 'Well, here we are at Wells Cathedral where the West Front represents the Last Judgement …' I've thought about that since and believe that is how people see God. They automatically, for some reason, assume there must be a judgement upon them. From the outside it seems as if he will judge, but it is not so, for the closer we come and the more we cast off our preoccupation with our painful condition, the more we will see that in God there is no wrath. For, as Julian says, 'For I saw no wrath except on man's side, and he forgives that in us, for wrath is nothing else but a perversity.' Or, as the prophet Zephaniah said some many hundreds of years earlier, 'The LORD has taken away the judgements against you.'

And that is a terrifying thought.

Part Four

The Passion of Christ

17

The 1940s House

'Do you not know that all of us who have been baptized into
Christ Jesus were baptized into his death?' (Romans 6.3)

There was a television series recently called *The 1940s House*.
In this a family of five volunteered to live for two months in
a house which was furnished as it would have been in the
1940s. They have 1940s heating and lighting, they have to
wear 1940s clothes, and live on a 1940s income with 1940s
food. For the purposes of the programme, a shop was created
where they could buy Bovril and Spam and blancmange for
$2^1/_2$d.

It was absolutely fascinating to see my childhood revived
before my very eyes. My family looked like that and listened
to radios like that. But it became even more fascinating as the
war developed and rationing was introduced and bread and
jam became a staple diet. Then what was called 'the Anderson
Shelter' arrived and the father had to dig up his back lawn to
erect this air raid shelter, and they all had to move into it when
the sirens went. You could see this family wishing that they
had never taken this on.

But it was a very interesting exercise for it brought to the
surface in a very vivid and dramatic way what was a defining
period of our history. It enabled people for whom it was a dim
childhood memory to live through in reality something which
had formed the psyche of our society. For the family concerned
it was a baptism by fire. They suddenly had to learn how to
make rissoles and wear corsets and do without television –

and they didn't like it. But it was also an entering into a defining experience, a participation of the baptism of our psyches. It was a way of entering into a formative story, the true story of our beginnings. This is what some theologians would call the myth of our origins. By this they do not mean something untrue or mythical, but something so profoundly true that it defines who we are, but which is hidden or buried deep within us. It was these years which formed my generation.

Other defining events form other generations of people. It is clear that the Vietnam war was a very defining period for Americans and has penetrated the national psyche in a particular way. The 1960s, along with the Beatles and miniskirts, has defined many of the cultural responses of another generation. And everybody knows where they were on the day President Kennedy was assassinated, and will remember where they were when the twin towers of the World Trade Centre were hit by hijacked aircraft.

But this is precisely what the baptism of Jesus was. It was a profoundly defining moment in his ministry, a moment which was of immense significance for him and which shaped his self-understanding and his teaching from that time onwards. It is one of the few events in Jesus' life which all four of the Gospels record. Significantly, all four Gospels record this event in terms of some sort of epiphany, an opening up of the divine in and for Jesus. And all four Gospels show that from that time on Jesus began his ministry teaching about the proximity of the rule of God, the nearness of the kingdom. This was the decisive event which shaped who he was and what he said. This was the turning point.

The comparison with the war years is very apt. These years were life-changing for us and for our society. They were totally devastating, but out of them emerged a new identity, a new way of being British, a new sort of society, and this new identity has shaped the thinking not just of those who survived it, but also that of their children, and their children. In a sense, it baptized a whole generation.

Now I've talked about baptism as a life-changing event, something deeply hidden within us like the war years, because I want to move away from understanding baptism as a sort of individual or personal decision, a choice which we make – or even which our parents make for us. Obviously it is that, it does involve our choice, but it is not simply an intellectual matter, the spiritual equivalent of choosing a new suit of clothes or a different suite of furniture. Baptism is not simply a choice you make; it is something which happens to you, it is something into which you enter and which changes who you are at the most profound level. The point is that this event does not leave you the same. Nor is it easy, as that family in the 1940s house found. It will involve change and loss, an abandonment of old ways, a movement out of one way of living into another. In very truth, in baptism, in the baptism of the people in the 1940s house, and in the baptism of Jesus and in our baptism, a new community is born. At the end of it all there is a new creation.

This is why when St Paul talks about baptism he talks about it as a sort of death. 'Do you not know that all of us who have been baptized into Christ Jesus were baptized into his death? Therefore we have been buried with him by baptism into death, so that just as Christ was raised from the dead by the glory of the Father, so we too might walk in newness of life' (Romans 6.3–4). In other words, being baptized was a participation in the death and the resurrection of Christ, it was an entry into a stripping and a renewal, a dying and a rising which was happening within you just as much as it happened historically to Christ himself on the cross. The parallel with the 1940s is exact. At that time there was a participation in a dying and a rising within us and within our descendants just as much as there was a historical dying and rising of British society.

And, for good measure, it was not just Paul who spoke

about the significance of baptism in these quasi cosmic terms, it was also Jesus himself. He spoke of his coming death as a baptism, and when James and John, two of his leading disciples, ask to sit at his side in the kingdom he says they do not know what they are asking. 'Are you able to drink the cup that I drink or be baptized with the baptism I am baptized with?' (Mark 10.38). He tells them that what is happening to him and they are asking to share is not just a pretty event with white robes and champagne. It is not just a television programme, not just another makeover, it is actually a participation in death in order to be reborn, and you are asking for more than you know.

That television programme was really an exploration of memory. Memory, what the New Testament calls *anamnesis* or remembering, is very much at risk in our modern society. Memories are thought by some to be controlling and authoritarian when really they give identity and community. In many ways the programme was an exploration of forgotten memories and of their importance. Each person who has been baptized has hidden deep within their psyche the memory of their baptism. Ostensibly a little event, a simple pouring of water in a church somewhere in the past, which is actually a life-changing, liberating, renewing event where the whole nature of things was changed for us.

Leading the Christian life is really a remembering, a delving deep into the significance of that little past event so that you realize just how life-giving, how cosmic, it was. Allowing the significance of that memory to surface and develop in our lives might well be like seeing ourselves as a photograph in a developing process. Gradually the true image will emerge, the emptiness of the modern will give way to the depth of image which is there, hidden and secret within us. The Christian life is the constant realization of that hidden secret. The process will involve a dying, but who we really are will come to life as never before.

When you pass through the waters, I will be with you;
and through the rivers, they shall not overwhelm
you;
When you walk through fire you shall not be burned,
and the flame shall not consume you.

For I am the LORD your God, the Holy One of Israel,
your Saviour...[1]

~18~

Things Fall Apart

'... *when you see these things taking place, you know that he
is near, at the very gates'* (Mark 13.29)

Reading St Mark's Gospel is not a gentle experience. If you
read it through it leaves you reeling. Not just punch-drunk
but blown away. At the end either you are broken open or you
close the book and say that is far too strenuous and difficult.
Part of it is the fast pace at which Jesus races through everything, with every event happening immediately upon its
predecessor with those repeated words, 'straightway,
straightway'. But there is also a clear sense of crisis hanging
over it all and which is focused in Chapter 13. Jesus predicts
the destruction of the temple and then, if you read on, you
hear of persecution, stars falling from heaven, and the coming
of the Son of Man on clouds from heaven. Everything is
broken open. And then, after that, there is the passion. This is
a stark and unrelenting narrative where the disciples fall

away and cannot face the terrible breaking that Christ calls them to. And the Gospel ends abruptly, 'and they said nothing to anyone, for they were afraid'. As one commentator says, 'The Gospel of Mark has a strong sense of an ending' – everything is coming to an end. Things are falling apart.

And trying to get hold of this and finding a way of talking to you about it I was put in mind of a performance of *King Lear* which I once saw. This is a very dramatic and moving play anyway, but all this was heightened in the production by setting it at a time of revolution in Europe. Lear was portrayed as a fading revolutionary leader who gives his country to his daughters, but really cannot abandon his power. This was vividly demonstrated in the staging. As the play progressed a great crack began to appear on the floor of the stage, a vivid black zig-zag which widened scene by scene until Lear went mad on the heath. At this point the crack opened wide and Lear stumbled into it along with the Fool and Mad Tom. It was a very telling device because the play is full of references to things breaking, breaking open, and stepping into darkness. You might remember the moving scene where Edgar leads his blind father to the edge of Dover cliff where he wants to step over into oblivion, but finds mercy.

Mark 13, indeed all of Mark's Gospel from Chapter 13 onwards, is not so very far from all this. As Jesus sits on the Mount of Olives musing over Jerusalem and the future it is as if he sees a great crack opening up, an ending coming. When you hear of wars and rumours of wars 'the sun will be darkened and the moon will not give its light'. Things are not right here, he says, it will all break up. There is another curious parallel between Mark's Gospel and the tragedy of *King Lear*. They both contain the strange sense that these endings are also beginnings, because they open up the possibilities of mercy. Gloucester has to step into the void in order to find the love of his son Edgar. Lear, the proud Lear, has to step into madness before he finds the forgiveness of his daughter, Cordelia, whom he had wronged. At this point, Lear tells her that, 'When thou dost ask me blessing, I'll kneel down and ask of thee forgiveness.'

And there is the same movement in Mark's Gospel. There Jesus does not simply predict disaster upon Jerusalem, but explicitly says, 'This is but the beginning of the birth pangs.' In other words, if you can endure it, if you can have the courage to step into the void, then you will be given new life. This is not simply disaster, but something good at work, something new being born of which you can be a part if you will. And at the end of Chapter 13, after he has predicted even greater disasters, Jesus says again that when the disaster comes this is actually an opportunity. 'When these things happen', he says, 'you know that summer is near. So keep awake, for you do not know when the time will come.'

What is being said here – directly by Jesus in St Mark's Gospel, and indirectly in *King Lear* – is that there are enormous forces at work in our lives. They are the profound forces of love and mercy which are at work by the power of God. The question is whether we will allow these enormous forces to break into our lives and carry us away. Can we allow the temple made with stones, the edifices of our own constructed self-made existence, to topple so that we can live by love and mercy? Can we live by the invisible power of God or not? What is constantly at work is God, but his activity is too much for us to bear; his reality, his forgiveness, appear so great that we take fright and cannot follow.

Religion isn't meant to make us feel good, it should not make us comfortable. Indeed, there is far too much comfortable religion around whereby people are lulled into a false and anodyne security and the Church is seen as the guardian of that. It is not that religion should make us unhappy, but the power of love is greater than anything we know. It blows things apart. If we allow it to work, then who or what we have made of ourselves will, properly speaking, come to an end.

That is why Lear's daughter Cordelia, the one who really loved him, would not speak of her love for him in cheap and easy terms such as those used by her sisters. That is why when Peter and the disciples protest their love for Jesus and say they want to follow him, he asks them whether they really know what they are talking about. Do they know both the joy and the passion of what love is? Will they bear the falling away of their false selves which following him will require? Will they bear the cross?

But the other point that is being made, both by Jesus in St Mark's Gospel and by the characters in *King Lear*, is that when you do allow this 'ending' to take place, then you will find within yourself a capacity for mercy and forgiveness such as you have never known before. Once you allow yourself to be broken, then you will find yourself carried along upon a great flood of the water of life, a torrent of beauty and goodness which will pour through you and carry you home. Only from the outside does the storm look as if it is the end of who you are. Once you have willingly entered it, ceased to resist the end, allowed your precious innermost citadel to be taken, your temple to be cast down, then you will know that what you have resisted was what you needed all along. Then you will weep tears over your own foolishness and lift your hands to welcome what you had feared. The moral of this is that when a terrible storm arises in your life, you must ask whether or not this storm is bringing you something you need. You have to assume that it does.

I have been reading the work of a young American woman theologian, Kathleen Norris. She was a poet living in New York who inherited family land in Dakota and returned there to live. She became a lay member of the order of St Benedict, even though she was a Presbyterian, and says that her attachment to the rule of St Benedict saved her marriage. In one of her books she describes how she was asked to preach to over a thousand people on Mark 13. She describes how at first she found all the imagery about the end-time very disturbing, but then realized that human beings 'seem to learn best how to live when we're a bit broken, when our plans fall apart, when our myths of self-sufficiency and goodness and safety are shattered. We then come to our senses and have a glimpse of what is possible, a glimpse of a new God-given way of being.'[1]

When the priest breaks the bread of the Eucharist and says, 'We break this bread to share in the body of Christ', it is not just bread which is broken, it is us. God's goodness and mercy then flows through the broken space, and 'We take upon us the mystery of things, as if we were God's spies.'[2]

~19~

The Fault Line

'I know that my Redeemer lives, and that at the last he will stand upon the earth' (Job 19.25)

Quite recently something happened to a friend of ours that I thought could never happen – something of major proportions which left us shocked and troubled. We talked about it quite a lot and I found myself saying that it was almost as if there were somebody else at work, somebody we didn't know about who had come through the person we knew and acted and spoken in a particular way. Perhaps even, it was somebody that the person themselves did not know was there, waiting in the background all these years, and then had suddenly marched through a life, knocking all the pieces flying.

One of the things this incident reminded me of was the vulnerability of human affairs, and the consequent necessity of simple and good things. It reminded me of the necessity for things like gratitude: gratitude for who we are and what we have, gratitude for those who love us, and gratitude for our work and daily food. Simple gratitude is healing and defeats evil. But I was also reminded that because human affairs are vulnerable we need to cherish each other, to be gentle with each other, to listen and to accompany each other through difficulties and dangers. We need to attend not just to what people say, but also to what they cannot say and are not saying to themselves as much as to you.

As I pondered our friend's predicament I was reminded that for all our sophistication, for all our education, for all our riches, darkness and the power and force of darkness is never very far away. It comes suddenly, takes us unawares, and before we know where we are we are not the person we thought we were. If you want to put theological language around all this you can easily do so, and I do not think that words like sin and redemption should be resisted. But I don't want to wrap it up in old language, we simply need to recognize what the Church has always said, and to speak of it fresh and clear and in the simplest possible way. The fault line is real, but the ultimate remedy comes from God.

The fault line is our hidden capacity to fall away from how we were created to be. That is why the phrase fault line is a good one, because you don't see it, and nor is it operative all of the time. We were created to be people of love and praise, people who live by means of the voice and love of God which speaks within them, people who by love and praise carry each other into the kingdom. And it is worth saying that this is not the same thing as happiness. People often say the purpose of life is happiness. I cannot see that, because pain and suffering cannot be avoided, whatever our contemporary culture tries to tell us. No, we are created to be people of love and praise who bear up and offer each other and all that is. We do this in company with Christ Jesus who constantly himself, in love and praise, bears the world back to the Father. But somehow our capacity to be people of love and praise falters. I think it falters for a number of reasons, but I believe it falters most often because we cannot be content with something so apparently simple. We think there must be something else, something more than this, something we do not have, something else we need to do or obtain. We think we need to steal fire from the gods because they have kept it for themselves and we, 'I', haven't got it. We have to make our way, shake off the old, get what we need. And it is at this point, when we stop being people of love and praise and want something more, that the Dark Man comes racing through our lives and overwhelms us with his blackness and scatters the pieces of our lives and other people's lives across the board. It is at this point that the hidden fault line decides to crack and we all fall down the hill.

In a sense, the origin of sin is a form of denial. Psychotherapists talk about living in denial when people are doing things, but not admitting to themselves what they are doing. We live in denial when we somehow cannot live with the simplicity of being people of love and praise, called back to being people of love and praise by the sacrificial love and praise of Christ our Redeemer. Being a person of love and praise should be enough for us. It is all you need; when we cannot accept that, the consequences are sometimes slight but potentially they are cataclysmic.

But I said earlier that I wanted to share two things, one that the fault line was real, and the second, that the ultimate remedy is God's.

Let me try and put this in context. More or less since the eighteenth century, Western intellectual life has been dominated by the view that human beings are essentially noble and responsible, who exercise free choice in accordance with reason, and are on a gradual march towards moral and spiritual perfection. And in all sorts of ways this overall view, this myth if you like, has guided us for nearly two hundred years and still guides much of what is said and done. All sorts of good things flow from this myth, but there is one thing about it which is difficult, and that is the question of fulfilment or perfectibility. We begin to think that we have the right to be fulfilled and that we can, provided we are careful, reach a degree of fulfilment ourselves.

All of this spills over into the way in which we talk about salvation in the Church. More and more, the language used about salvation implies that it is something to be worked at and holiness is something which Christians are urged to achieve. The means of this self-perfecting holiness are dangled before us. I know this is a caricature, but I was once in the dentist's waiting room leafing through the magazines and found a long pull-out supplement on the way to wholeness or something similar. After the usual articles about diet and exercise and the importance of fibre and jogging, I turned the page to find a section on 'spiritual health' with a list of retreat houses and the importance of meditation. Religion had become the ultimate fashion accessory.

But the way of life to which we are called involves an acknowledgement of my own inability to perfect myself and a basic acknowledgement that while I am called to co-operate with God's grace my life will only be holy because of his gift, his grace. There is in the end some sort of radical differentness about God. He is not just the super-human being. This differentness is only bridged from his side, but it is bridged, and grace does undergird all of life. What we find difficult to accept in our modern condition is the utter otherness and holiness of God and that nothing we do or say can command him. His mercy, his grace, his forgiveness is what enlivens and fills the universe. There is a secret, hidden life which reaches out to catch and transform and it is God's hidden, secret gift.

The other day I remembered, I thought rather late, that I had to go into the cathedral in which I work to speak to someone. I came in suddenly to hear the well-known soprano, Emma Kirkby, rehearsing for a performance of Handel's *Messiah* that evening. She had just reached the final soprano aria, 'I know that my Redeemer liveth and that he shall stand at the last day'. The whole cathedral was transfixed by her singing. Nobody moved, all the visitors stopped walking about and just sat down. The absolute clarity and beauty of her line seemed to come from somewhere else. I was brought up short. I couldn't move, indeed I found myself fighting back tears, quite overcome. It was a message of grace suddenly given. It said all would be well.

I wanted our friend to hear it.

~20~

The Passion of Our Lord Jesus Christ According to St Mark[1]

If we read through the passion of Jesus in St Mark's Gospel, we can, perhaps by a trick of the imagination, find ourselves caught up in the drama of Jesus of Nazareth and his disciples. Fearful, sometimes terrified, we can follow these events as Jesus, the dissident preacher from the north, is arrested, tried and executed. We can watch, drawn as it were by a mighty power, by divine attraction, and become part of what is going on. In the end what was happening then will become, as we follow, what is happening to us now, and we will know God's power and presence in our lives.

1   The Anointing (Mark 14.3–10)

In St Mark's Gospel the passion and suffering of Jesus begins
with this incident of the anointing of Jesus by a woman. We
might find that surprising and think to ourselves, 'No, he's
got that wrong, surely the passion and suffering of Jesus
began when he came into Jerusalem on a donkey and cleared
the temple of the money-changers?' Doesn't it say, back in
Chapter 11, three chapters before this little story, that 'When
they heard about it they kept looking for a way to kill him'?
That is true, and in one sense the incident at the temple sealed
Jesus' death politically speaking, but this little private, domestic incident with the woman at supper inside somebody's
house is the real beginning because it is here that the enormity
and the grace of what was going on began to make an impact
upon the interior lives of the disciples. It was at this point they
began to realize that something enormous and powerful,
something life-changing, was going on.

This is a very domestic incident. It takes place in Bethany,
just outside Jerusalem over the Mount of Olives, where Jesus
is known to have stayed during his last week. The same story
occurs in St John's Gospel, and there the domestic and intimate setting of the story is heightened even further. There it
takes place in the house of Lazarus, whom Jesus had raised
from the dead, and there it is not an unknown woman who
anoints Jesus but Mary, Lazarus' sister. This only emphasizes
what is already present in St Mark's Gospel: that this is an
incident which happens *inside*, inside a house, and inside the
hearts of those who are present. This is a spiritual action, a
spiritual moment. As you read St Mark's Gospel you become
aware that there are two 'places' where Jesus acts. There are
public places, where healings and exorcisms take place, and
then there are private places, where special intimate things
happen, where the disciples are instructed, and where special
revelations occur. It is also in these private places, many of

them indoors, where Jesus meets a number of women, and where the insight of these women is seen to be greater than that of his disciples. We think of St Luke's Gospel as being the one about women, but St Mark's Gospel also shows them coming into their own at pertinent points. St Mark has the Syrophoenician woman in Chapter 7, the one who has a daughter with an unclean spirit and who dares to face out Jesus over the question of Jewish priority. That incident occurs 'inside', and there are a number of others. This is an incident like that. While we often think of St Mark's Gospel as being dramatic and active and somewhat masculine with everything happening immediately, there are also in St Mark a number of the contrasting and intimate moments where women are involved, and they demonstrate that they know more about what is really going on. So this incident with the ointment is like that, an incident which reflects what is really going on which only the woman had the insight to see.

Several facets of this story are luminous. First of all, it is an unknown woman. She is not named. In St John's account the woman is Mary, Lazarus' sister. This woman seems to come from nowhere, she is a force rather than an individual. And she anoints his head, again a very powerful symbol for in Jewish thinking an anointing on the head was an anointing for kingship. And third, she pours out the whole box, not just a few drops but the whole of it. The incident represents an extraordinary portrayal of generosity coming out from a very deep place.

Jesus receives her gift. He does not turn her away as deluded or a bit too close for comfort. He receives her and what she does. He says, 'She has anointed me for burial.' He recognizes that this is a preparation for death. He says she knows what is going on here, she is aware of what is about to happen and is ready for it. Jesus interprets the action as a preparation for burial, the burial of a king, and so as a sign that this woman had recognized what was going on and was making him ready for his role as the king who would suffer.

We should reflect upon the immense generosity of this woman's gift. It is more than a generous action, it is a deeply expansive action, it is a total gesture of love and devotion which seems to come almost from nowhere. This unknown woman, by doing this, shows that she is aware of, and in touch with, the inner significance of Jesus' presence in Jerusalem. It is as if she knows that he is the embodiment of the over-whelming grace of God poured out in love for the world. It is as if she has seen what he is and, by symbolically anointing him, imitates with her action what God is doing in and through him. She is saying, 'Yes, there is an enormous explosion and outpouring of life in you, a life which will carry you through death. I am pouring this precious ointment over you because you are precious, because you are going to die, because your life enfolds and upholds all of our deaths.' So this apparently private incident is the beginning of Jesus' passion, because here the enormity and grace of what was going on in Jesus begins to make its impact upon the interior lives of the disciples. The woman saw an outpouring of immense love which enfolds death, and symbolized that in her action.

But the disciples cannot bear it. They are shocked and disturbed. They do not like what is happening and talk about the waste of money that is involved. 'Why was the ointment wasted in this way? For this ointment could have been sold for more than three hundred denarii and the money given to the poor.' And in one sense they had a point, because the Torah made people responsible for the poor particularly at Passovertide. But, as Jesus says, that is a universal law, you will always be responsible for the poor, so why haven't you done something about that already? Your protest, he implies, is a disguise for your shock and disturbance because what is really going on here is your failure to see that God is at work. What you have failed to see this unknown woman has seen. So Jesus receives her gift, but rebukes the disciples for making pious noises about the poor when really they too should have been ready to pour their love and their gratitude out upon him.

Increasingly in Mark's Gospel the disciples are seen to be empty followers, too frightened, too disturbed, by what is going on to make a ready response to it. As the story of Jesus' passion unfolds, the disciples are seen to be increasingly in disarray, increasingly distant from what is happening. The signs are there earlier in the Gospel where he sets his face to go to Jerusalem and they follow in dismay. And, we shall see, as we read on, how they fall away until only Peter follows at a distance, and then even he cannot sustain his loyalty. The enormity of what is going on is too great. But there are others who take the disciples' place, like this woman, who give all they can find to honour his sacrifice. She, of course, presents disturbing questions for us and our lack of ability to pour out love. In the face of her example, all our disguises fall away. We too will speak pious words about the poor, whom we should be supporting anyhow, but give little in recognition of the need to welcome and honour the King of Glory among us now, calling us to sacrifice our lives.

2   The Sleep of the Disciples (Mark 14.32–42)

Jesus leaves the Upper Room where he had supper with his disciples and they go out across the valley between Jerusalem and the Mount of Olives to a spot they have used in the past as a place to gather and meet and reflect on what is happening. There Jesus takes his three favoured disciples, Peter, James and John, and goes on to pray. There is a sense of impending disaster hanging over the scene as night falls.

Before all this, Jesus had spoken to his disciples about the coming of the Son of Man. He said there would be false claims and false prophets, so the disciples would have to be alert and watchful. In the end, he says, only God knows the time of the final hour: 'Beware, keep alert; for you do not know when the time will come.' And then, twice, he tells his disciples to stay awake, 'Keep awake, for you do not know when the master of the house will come... Keep awake.'

But now, even at the crucial hour, the disciples do fall asleep. So, first of all, this scene is not just something that happened. It is preceded, only a page or so previously, by the strenuous warnings of Jesus to the disciples to 'stay awake', and so is clearly intended to make a point. He had told them and now they didn't. And then, in addition, the same point is emphasized within the story itself. Jesus tells them to stay awake, and then comes back three times and each time finds them sleeping. The disciples fail to heed their Master's command.

But a further point is made. Jesus is shown as leaving the body of the disciples and taking Peter, James and John on with him deeper into the Garden of Gethsemane. You may remember that he has done this before. He did it when he restored Jairus' daughter to life in Chapter 5. Again in Chapter 9, he took Peter, James and John up the mountain, 'Apart and by themselves', and he was transfigured before them. There they saw how he is linked to Elijah and Moses, two figures who in popular Jewish understanding were righteous men who endured great suffering. So already Peter and James and John have been told by Jesus that suffering is the role of the righteous. But, of course, this is something they have consistently rejected. Peter had rejected Jesus' prediction about the passion in Chapter 8. He took Jesus aside and told him not to talk like that, but Jesus rebuked him and talked about the importance of taking up your cross. James and John are shown as wanting to have places of power and honour when Jesus comes into his kingdom, and they blatantly say they can drink 'the cup' that Jesus will drink. But their words are hollow. 'The cup', of course, is the cup of suffering and now, in the Garden, faced with this cup, these three leading disciples are all shown to fail. They fall asleep; not once, but three times. So the way the story is told not only emphasizes how falling asleep is a failure to observe Jesus' earlier command to stay awake; it also emphasizes how the three leading disciples, the ones whom Jesus had confided in most closely and who had already been told what was in store, show themselves to have totally failed to understand what was going on in his ministry. At the crucial point it seems they fall into oblivion, they cannot bear what they see.

So what is really going on here? What is really going on is that Jesus' disciples – even the three leading disciples – are shown as falling away from their Lord in the time of trial. They cannot face the requirement that the Son of Man suffer. Sleep is, of course, a way of dealing with great suffering, but here this sleep is the sleep of forgetfulness, it is a deep resistance to the way of discipleship which Jesus, the one who will suffer (just as so many righteous ones suffered in the past), calls them to follow.

The Christian way is the very opposite of sleep and forgetfulness; it is the way of remembering. Christians are those who remember who they are before God and who come together, Sunday by Sunday, to remember Jesus and his way. They celebrate the holy mysteries and 'remember' his life and ministry, his teaching, his suffering and death and resurrection, and by so doing, week by week, are in turn 're-membered' by God. He 're-members' us and puts us back together again, puts our fragmented disordered consciousnesses back into the pattern in which they were created.

'Forgetfulness' – which is another name for the sleep of the disciples – is that failure which allows us to turn away from the responsibilities of truth, allows us to deny or 'forget' what is really going on while we live in another world. We might live in a dream or in a fantasy all of our own, an illusion which is safer and easier to endure than the truth or the reality to which God calls us.

The modern world is particularly good at providing us with fantasies which protect us from reality. Our society is characterized by forgetfulness. We forget death, we forget the past. Those of us who live in the West can easily 'forget' the plight of the two-thirds world or the plight of the disabled within our own land. Those who are different are not seen.

When I was the director of a conference centre we used to host training events for social workers. They would be sent out into a nearby town in a wheelchair as if they were disabled to observe at first hand what the obstacles were for such people. The worst thing they said was people's 'lack of seeing'. We sleep to that which we do not want. In so doing, the cross is perpetuated in our society. One of our contemporary Christian poets says that the modern human condition is very much 'a sleep': 'We have forgotten our true selves, we have been lulled by a false consciousness, by modern waters of Lethe, into a sleep which we mistake for reality. We might prefer to forget because sleep is easier and less demanding and sometimes less painful than wakefulness – which is nevertheless that to which we must grow.'[2]

Jesus is the great awakener. He shows us the reality of ourselves before God. When he wakes the disciples he tells them to pray. Prayer is, essentially, that which keeps us awake because it exposes us – and exposes that for which we pray – to the truth which is God. Prayer is a self-exposure to the gaze of God; it is a presentation of ourselves and the world of which we are a part to the searching, ever-loving, ever-wakeful eye of God, who by his gaze destroys our fantasies and wakens us, for: 'When I awake I shall see thee as thou art' (Psalm 17.16, AV).

3 The Betrayal by Judas (Mark 14.43–50)

So we come to the point where Jesus is betrayed by Judas Iscariot, arrested by the authorities, and taken away for trial.

We might spend some time imagining this event – the disciples and Jesus in the Garden; the fact that it happened at night, deepening the sense of impending disaster. Then, in the darkness, the clink of arms and the voices. Judas perhaps saying quietly 'Over here', and then the final rapid arrest and the flight of the disciples. And we might, if we are so inclined, spend some time reflecting on the person of Judas and what caused him to betray his Master. Was it money? Was it disappointed hope? Had he wanted Jesus to be a revolutionary leader? Did he want to be part of the senior management team – up there with Peter, James and John – but wasn't picked out?

There is a long tradition, from Ignatius Loyola onwards, which encourages scripture readers to reflect upon what they see in their mind's eye and to meditate upon what is happening – the motivation, for example, of Judas in betraying Jesus. And the purpose of such reflection, of course, is to enable people to reflect upon their own motivations in life, and to cleanse them from pride and jealousy or power-seeking by showing that such things were part of what brought Jesus to the cross in the first place. But there is real risk in such a process. For however much we might reflect, say, on motivation, that is not really part of the account in the Gospels as we have it. There is no speculation here about Judas' motives. Indeed, there is almost a sense that what happened would have happened anyway, almost independently of Judas' motives. Judas' personal motives are not mentioned. It is more something which Judas has to do. Indeed, in St John's Gospel Jesus is portrayed as knowing who it was that would hand him over and actually, by giving Judas the piece of bread, told him to get on with it. In St Mark's account, Jesus says as he is arrested 'let the scriptures be fulfilled'. So Judas' personal motivation is not regarded as important by the Gospel writers. He is regarded as the trigger or the fulcrum for something bigger. There were, the Gospels are saying, enormous forces at work here which used Judas so that, effectively, God's work could be done. The scriptures had to be fulfilled.

This impression is confirmed when you look at the words which the Gospel writers use. We easily use the word 'betray' to describe what Judas did, and that word has all sorts of implications such as 'ill will' and 'evil intent'. But the Greek is not so ambiguous. There are two Greek words: *prodidomi*, which means to betray and is deliberate, and *paradidomi*, which means 'to hand over'. It is this word which is used almost without exception by the Gospel writers, as well as by Paul, when they talk about the death of Jesus. That death is always 'a handing over'. John says, 'Jesus bowed his head and handed over his spirit.' So whereas *paradidomi* in English becomes *betray*, in the Greek it is much more colourless and really means something much more passive such as 'hand over'. Judas is the one who hands Jesus over. Judas is known as 'the hander over' and we should note that this is all he is. The Gospels do not describe him in any more emotive ways such as 'the secret enemy' or 'the informer', or anything of that kind.

Then we have to reckon with the way St Mark describes Jesus during all this. We all know that the Gospel writers exhibit different characteristics and show different aspects of Jesus' ministry. St Mark's Gospel shows the active Jesus. He is always on the move, always doing, always speaking, never still. Everything is immediate. But the remarkable thing is that once Jesus is handed over by Judas to the authorities then all that suddenly stops. Jesus does not act, he is acted upon. He hardly speaks, except to respond to other people – 'You have said so' and so on.

So at this point in the passion, as Judas hands Jesus over to the authorities, Jesus becomes the one who is acted upon rather than the one who acts. He becomes the patient rather than the active healer. He becomes the one who undergoes the passion. St John in his account of the arrest of Jesus makes this explicit when he says that immediately upon his arrest Jesus was bound.

What does all this mean? It means that it is in the nature of God to hand himself over in love, and in love to wait upon our response. If God is love, truly love, then his love is not manipulative, it does not control our response. It gives itself patiently and is 'bound' by our response to it. We may or may not accept the offer of God's love to us. If God's love were such that it somehow controlled or manipulated our response, then it would not be pure love. So it is in Christ. He pours himself out in love towards us in such a way that waits upon our response. That demonstrates the totality of his love, the almost desperate quality of what God is constantly doing. He needs, he calls for our response, but waits to see what we will do. God is the waiting lover.

Much of human loving is less than this. We will love provided there is a response. We will only wait so long; we will only love when we know we are loved in return. We appear to be only able to give if there is some return on our giving, only give aid if the poor do what we want with our gifts. In God, there is no such restraint. He hands himself over totally in generosity to us. 'He who did not withhold his own Son but gave him up for all of us, will he not with him also give us everything else?' (Romans 8.32)

Handing yourself over is costly, but that is what God does and, in Christ, calls us all to share if we are to live.

4 The Denial of Peter (Mark 14.66–72)

At the end of the Last Supper with his disciples, as they went out to the Mount of Olives, Jesus had predicted that they would all become deserters and leave him. He even quoted Zechariah, '… strike the shepherd, and the sheep will be scattered', to prove his point. Peter, however, is emphatic in his denials: 'Even if everybody else deserts you I won't', and

Jesus makes his prediction that before the night is out and the cock has crowed twice in the early morning light, Peter will have denied him three times.

We are told that as Jesus is led away Peter followed at a distance and sat warming himself with the guards. But it is not until after Jesus' testimony before the Sanhedrin that the crisis occurs. He is accused of being a follower of Jesus. He denies it, tries to move away into the forecourt; but is accused again, denies it again; is accused again, and then, after a third denial, hears the cock crow. He then realizes what he has done.

So Peter, who had followed him enthusiastically, who led the disciples in affirming him as the Messiah, who crept undetected right into the inner court, now even he denies him. Jesus' insight was correct, 'You will all fall away because of me.' Gradually the disciples he called to follow him had all deserted him. At first they simply resist the call to go to Jerusalem; Peter had tried to persuade Jesus that his talk of going there to die was a nonsense, but then as the events in Jerusalem unfold even Peter denies him. At the end of the Gospel, at his resurrection, even the women who go to the tomb to anoint his body run away 'for terror and amazement had seized them'.

In explanation of all this, the biblical commentators tell us that St Mark's Gospel was written against a background of persecution. The purpose of the Gospel was to strengthen the faith of the Christian community by showing that from the beginning they will have to endure suffering and even martyrdom. The message of Jesus was clear: his disciples must remember that God will sustain them in conflict, and the Son of Man will appear to establish God's rule on earth. The Gospel was written to say that whereas the first disciples faced persecution just as you do now, do not fall away as they did.

That is the standard interpretation. But I wonder whether there is not more to it than that.

What we have to become aware of is a deeper significance. St Mark shows that the disciples were being faced with the reality of God in Jesus. They had thought that this was a reality they could cope with – they followed, initially, confident in their leader. Perhaps they thought they were following a teacher who gave them a new perspective on Jewish teaching, but no more than that. As things develop, however, the disciples begin to realize that Jesus' intentions are greater than they realized. He wants to go to Jerusalem and is talking about the possibilities of death. As they follow him to Jerusalem it might have dawned upon them that Jesus is not just another teacher, but somehow, mysteriously, embodies much more. In and through the horror of those last days the majesty and the overwhelming terrible reality of God is shown to be present.

I say 'terrible', but only in the sense that something is terrible because you fear it. If you turn and embrace this fear, Jesus implies, then you will find yourself embraced by the overwhelming love and mercy of God. That is the agony which Jesus faces in the Garden and that is the agony he calls his disciples to share. 'Can you drink the cup that I will drink?' Oh yes, of course we can, they reply, but in the event they do not.

In his dying, Jesus calls us to take up the cross daily and follow him. What this means is that we are called to a constant internal process of letting go, a constant acceptance of loss as the way to life. We have to accept that we, our own egos, our own selves are not the centre of the universe. We have to die to self. We have to allow our own ego-selves to fall away and accept that we are lovingly and beautifully constituted in God and God alone. But not only that, we also have to die to 'this world'. This is a particular concern of the author of St John's Gospel. But 'this world' does not mean the world as created. We are called to die to 'this world', which is that complex set of forces to which we have given our loyalty and which, we think, keeps us in being. 'This world' is the complex set of associations and networks which we have erected to give us identity and security. These are those networks of ambition, of self-aggrandisement, of materialism and greed, which we think we need. In the end we need none of these and they all have to fall away. To die to the self and to die to this world is what Jesus called his disciples to do.

This letting go, this acceptance of loss, is not a negative matter. It appears a negative matter from this side of the cross, but from the other side it is stepping into the immense and overwhelming reality of God. For the disciples, this reality came too close and they became deeply fearful and turned away.

This is what happened to Peter. By following Jesus into the Praetorium he follows him into the darkness, into the arena of death. But he wants to do it in an unrecognized way. He wants to be there unseen. From the way the story is told he is shown as knowingly coming with Jesus to the heart of things. He will follow, he knows that there is some reality here which draws him, in spite of his fears, into the darkest arena. But he cannot allow himself to be recognized. He cannot, as Jesus does, own his presence, throw off his cloak, and stand free. At the last minute he denies ownership. Which of us has not been in that place? It is as if Peter, when Jesus looks at him, is faced with the immensity, the overwhelming dazzling darkness, the great reality of God, and knows, at last, what it is that he has been following. But by then it is too late.

This poem by Charles Causley could be addressed to Peter:

I am the great sun, but you do not see me,
I am your husband, but you turn away.
I am the captive, but you do not free me,
I am the captain you will not obey.

I am the truth, but you will not believe me,
I am the city where you will not stay

I am your wife, your child, but you will leave me,
I am that God to whom you will not pray.

I am your counsel, but you do not hear me,
I am the lover whom you will betray,
I am the victor, but you do not cheer me
I am the holy dove whom you will slay.

I am your life but if you will not name me
Seal up your soul with tears, and never blame me.[3]

5   Dying

We have followed Jesus from the point where an unknown
woman anointed him with a costly ointment, through the
Garden of Gethsemane and the sleep of the disciples, through
the point where Judas Iscariot handed him over to the authorities and then on to his trial where we watched, horrified,
as Peter denied his friend. And while we followed these
events as history, we have also become aware that in them
something more was going on. This something more was of
God.

What we have seen in and through these events as St
Mark's account tells them is the gradual falling away of the
disciples. They find they cannot follow Christ to the end. This
falling away begins with grumbling at the waste of the
precious ointment poured over Jesus by the unknown woman.
They go on to fall asleep when he most needs their support,
and then they turn away. Judas cannot bear it any more and
hands him over and the rest flee for their lives. Peter clings on
a bit longer, drawn to Jesus' side, but then even he, the faithful
friend, denies that he knew him. Jesus said 'You will all fall
away from me this night', and they all denied it. But they did,
and in the end he was left alone and in his solitude con-
demned to death. He was stripped of his clothes and his

dignity and then crucified, publicly disposed of. Slowly, sear-ingly, thirstily, hated, alone, he died. St Mark's Gospel tells us that while he died it became dark, and at the end Jesus gave a great cry of desolation and loneliness: 'My God, my God, why have you forsaken me?' He dies in deep desolation, abandoned not just by his disciples, but also by God himself.

Why does St Mark write about it all like this? It is not just the story of a man who is abandoned by his friends at the last minute. It is really a story about absence. It is about the absence of friends at the last minute, but then more than that, it is about the absence of God. God is apparently not there, he has hidden himself away. Even a cursory glance through the scriptures will show that this profound sense of absence or hiddenness is not uncommon. It begins with Moses, to whom God says, 'You cannot see my face' (Exodus 33.20), because if you saw my face you would not live. It continues in the Psalms and in Isaiah: 'Truly, you are a God who hides himself' (Isaiah 45.15). It is there in Job, the symbol of all who suffer without reason. 'If I go forward,' he says, 'he is not there; or backward, I cannot perceive him' (Job 23.8). Job, Isaiah, Jeremiah in the Lamentations, all prefigure and echo Jesus on the cross. 'Truly you are a God who hides yourself. You do not appear to be there.'

But is it darkness? Is it absence? Or could it not rather be understood in a different way? Could it not be better under-stood as the death of our own images of God. Perhaps in this process of dying Jesus is leading us away from our own self-constructed view of God and into the depth of his beauty, a beauty which is such that in it 'I', and all that 'I' want, is consumed and burned away? In reflecting on Peter's denial I suggested that Peter denied Christ because he was actually in retreat from something, something that gropingly he knew he needed, but at that stage could not face. He was afraid of too much light. So, as he gets closer and closer to the light and what it requires of him, he turns away. So he denies his Lord because he cannot face the enormity of God. As we saw, Charles Causley put it so well in his poem: 'I am the great sun, but you do not see me, I am your husband, but you turn away.' Faced with the realization of what God in Christ might require, and the death of their selves that this would involve, the disciples all fall away. Jesus, on the contrary, goes on into the darkness and ultimately accepts the death of his self and the illusions of the self that is required of those who would see God. He asks, in the Garden of Gethsemane, 'Does it have to be this way?', but in the end accepts the absence because he knows that God is greater than anything he can know or say or experience. The absence is a signpost to the future.

There is no doubt that the darkness is real, that death has to be accepted, and that there is in Jesus, and in those who follow him to the end, a desolation of the soul. But in the end it will be the death of a self we thought was ours, the death of our illusory and selfish lives, the death of what St John called 'this world', the complex web of selfish desire and selfish support that we give ourselves in this life in order to prove to ourselves that we are real. Dying to all of this is real and very hard because we build up an identity, a reality for ourselves, thinking that without it we will not live. When you look at the earth from space the lights we create never go out. We do not appear to be able to bear the dark. But Jesus, faced with the reality of God – the Great Sun – does not turn away. He accepts the dazzling darkness and dies to his own 'seeing' of things in order to be 'seen' only by God.

All this is put more carefully in another poem, *The Hound of Heaven* by Francis Thompson. The poet begins by feeling pursued. Like the disciples, he flees from the divine presence. It could be Peter speaking:

> I fled him, down the nights and down the days;
> I fled him, down the arches of the years;
> I fled him down the labyrinthine ways
>   of my own mind, and in the midst of tears
> I hid from him.[4]

But then, at the end of the poem, God calls to the poet and says all that which you thought you had lost is stored up for you. 'Rise, clasp my hand and come'. The poet responds: 'Halts by me, that footfall? Is my gloom, after all, shade of his hand, outstretched caressingly?'

And that is it. Jesus answers yes to that question and enters the apparent gloom to take his Father's hand and retrieve his heritage. The question his death poses for us is whether we can do the same and die. Can we die to our dreams of success, our desire to see by our own eyes? 'If any want to become my followers, let them deny themselves and take up his cross and follow me.'

> He is that great void
> we must enter, calling
> to one another on our way
> in the direction from which
> he blows. What matter
> if we should never arrive
> to breed or to winter
> in the climate of our conception?
> Enough we have been given wings
> and a needle in the mind
> to respond to his bleak north.
> There are times even at the Pole
> When he too pauses in his withdrawal
> so that it is light there all night long.[5]

Part Five

Risen, Ascended, Glorified

~21~

The Anointing of Jesus in John

*'If I, your Lord and Teacher, have washed your feet, you also
ought to wash one another's feet' (John 13.14)*

The other day I was invited to a book launch. The book was
called *The Last Supper According to Martha and Mary*[1] and was
written by a Roman Catholic woman friend. It is a retelling of
the Easter story from the point of view of Mary and Martha,
the two sisters of Lazarus, a sort of imaginative reconstruction. It shows the passionate nature of these two women's
involvement with Jesus and the disciples. There are some
very interesting insights which are well worth reading, and
when it comes to describing the Last Supper and the
footwashing of the disciples, it tells how Jesus not only
washes the feet of his male disciples, but his female ones as
well. Mary describes her feelings as Jesus washes her feet:
'And now, at last, Jesus kneels at my feet. I have been washing
men's feet since childhood, but never before has a man
washed my feet … Is this a secret ritual that we share, he and
I? Caught up in the swirl of memories, I think of the other
night when I washed his feet, and the moment is suffused
with intimacy … I remember the smell of the perfume I used
to anoint him, and I close my eyes and it is as if the fragrance
still lingers between us and enfolds us like a lover's embrace.'

You might think, reading all that, that the book is a sort of
religious Mills and Boon novel, a bit tawdry perhaps; but a
careful look at the New Testament text will show that the
author was not far off the mark. There is an explicit link in

St John's Gospel between the story of the anointing of Jesus by Mary in Chapter 12 and the washing of the disciples' feet, which John places during the Last Supper in Chapter 13. In the book I've been reading Mary remembers the anointing she gave Jesus when he washes her feet. In St John's Gospel the story of the anointing precedes and prefigures the foot-washing.

Let's just pause for a moment to see how this happens. There are three different accounts of the anointing of Jesus in the New Testament. Mark – who is very closely followed by Matthew – shows Jesus anointed by an unknown woman, but the ointment is poured over Jesus' head. Mark says this is a preparation for burial. Luke, however, shows Jesus anointed on his feet, but there is no linkage with Jesus' death; indeed, the incident happens long before Jesus ever begins his journey to Jerusalem. John takes elements from both of these accounts – the anointing of Jesus' feet from Luke is linked to Mark's emphasis on the anointing as a prefiguring for burial – and creates a new account of the incident altogether. He also moves the story right forward in time so that it occurs a week before Passover and the woman is named as Mary, the sister of Martha and Lazarus.

John wants to show us that there is a parallel between Mary's anointing of Jesus' feet as an act of love and service and his washing of the disciples' feet as an act of love and service. In other words, she prefigures his action and so models what he will do. Even the words of the two incidents are similar, with the same emphasis upon *wiping* – she *wiped* Jesus' feet with her hair, he *wiped* the disciples' feet with a towel.

So my friend's imaginative reconstruction of the Last Supper with Mary having her feet washed by Jesus, and remembering her own washing of his feet is not so very far from the mark. The two events are explicitly linked in John's Gospel – the one points forward to the other.

And thereby hangs the meaning. In the footwashing, Jesus will wash his disciples' feet as an expression of his love for them. He asks them to do this for each other. 'If I, your Lord and teacher, have washed your feet, you also ought to wash one another's feet.' But all this Mary has already done for him. Mary has already, in her anointing, demonstrated the discipleship which he calls for from them all a week later.

She has already shown herself to be the model of discipleship. She is the one, not Peter, not any of the others, who demonstrates what discipleship really means.

That is the reason why John names Judas as the objector in his account. In St Mark it was simply 'some' who objected to this woman's behaviour. In St Luke it is the Pharisees, but in John it is Judas, the anti-disciple, the non-disciple. John wants to draw an explicit contrast between the model discipleship of Mary and the scorn and betrayal of Judas. She is the one who knows what it really means.

But there was also an earlier incident where Mary showed herself to be the loyal disciple. She, it seems, knows the way of discipleship instinctively, for when Jesus comes to raise Lazarus from the dead she is portrayed as responding to his call before she even knows what he wants. She moves then immediately in response, just as now, in this anointing; it is not just ointment she pours over his feet, but also herself.

Discipleship is defined by acts of love and devotion. It is not defined – at least not here in this story – by choice or by particular acts of commitment. It is not an act of deliberate choice, it is an act of passion. The true disciple, John seems to be saying, is the one who, like Mary, pours themselves out in total passion for this man. In the light of this, choice, or discipleship as a chosen following, an act of the will, fades into insignificance. And it is worth noting that St John's Gospel does not contain the same stories of 'the Twelve' and their following of Jesus. Indeed, 'the Twelve' as an ecclesiastical grouping, with Peter at its head, very much fades into the background in John by comparison with the other Gospels. This group with Peter at its head hardly appears, and Peter is hardly a star figure. It is not Peter upon whom Christ builds his Church, but Mary. Mary is the model for what counts; and what counts, John is saying, is her capacity for passion and friendship, passionate friendship. That will carry us through death. Jesus talks about laying down his life for his friends – not for some cause, not for something you do not know, but for the people you know and love, and here is Mary pouring her best self all over this man. Christianity is not a choice, not a reasoned faith, not a cleverness – it is a passion, and only with a passion will you be saved.

What will carry us through Holy Week and bring us out into the Garden on the other side is the passion of Mary. Her love and passion carry her through. You see, I suspect that the Church doesn't understand passion very easily. We are obsessed with reconstruction and management causes of one kind or another, and while these things have their place, they will not reconstruct the Church or stop its decline. To do that we have to bear within ourselves the loving passionate friendship of Mary for her Lord. And that is why my friend's book is so right – for there Mary is a disciple, the disciple, but the disciple because she loved this man and gave herself to him.

So when you think to yourself each year, 'How shall I observe Easter?', don't say, 'Do I understand the atonement?' Don't say to yourself, 'Have I worked out why Jesus died? Do I believe it?' Don't even say to yourself, 'Have I gone to church enough? Do I belong enough?' Don't ask yourself ecclesiastical questions at all. Above all, don't ask moral questions about whether you are good enough, whether you have obeyed enough. No, don't ask those questions at Easter. Ask yourself instead whether you are a lover. Ask yourself whether you can love much. Ask yourself whether you would follow this man, pour out your nard upon him. Ask yourself whether your passion will sustain you – kill you, yes, but sustain you

– through your death and his so that you too can await him in
the Garden on Easter morning.

Set me as a seal upon your heart,
    as a seal upon your arm;
for love is strong as death,
    passion fierce as the grave.
Its flashes are flashes of fire,
    a raging flame.
Many waters cannot quench love
neither can floods drown it.[2]

~22~

Ascension as Absence

*'Do not hold on to me, because I have not yet ascended to the
Father' (John 20.17)*

When I was a parish priest in London my parish included
one of our major public schools, and on Ascension Day it
was the school's custom to hold a great service in their
chapel and invite their neighbouring clergy to the service
and then lunch with the headmaster afterwards. This was
always a splendid occasion – and on one of these I found
myself at lunch next to the headmaster's wife with the
morning's preacher opposite. He had preached a fine sermon, so I congratulated him and said how pleased I was that
he had not portrayed Jesus on Ascension Day as taking off
from the earth like a rocket from Cape Canaveral. 'But oh,'

said the headmaster's wife, 'Oh, Mr Matthews, isn't that what we are supposed to believe …?'

We might chuckle, but the story raises for us the question of the significance of the ascension for Christian believing. What is it all about? I want to say that the ascension of Christ is a parable of the centrality of *absence* for Christian belief and discipleship. It is an affirmation, indeed a celebration, of the absence of Jesus of Nazareth. Christians are asked, by this great feast, not just to tolerate the fact that Jesus has gone – been taken away from them as the scripture puts it – but actually to celebrate that absence, to rejoice in it as the means by which their lives – and indeed the life of the whole world – is filled with joy. What the ascension is not about is movement upwards. It was the headmaster's wife's mistake, and maybe ours, to concentrate upon that and to puzzle about how that happened. It is not about physical movement, it is about absence and the appropriation of absence.

Look for a moment if you will at the New Testament accounts of the ascension and what is happening to the people involved in those accounts. The primary witness, of course, is Mary Magdalene, who finds the risen Jesus in the garden on the first Easter Day. She is so overwhelmed by her meeting with Jesus that she embraces him. Jesus rebukes her and says 'Do not hold on to me … I am ascending to my Father and your Father' (John 20.17). And a little later the same happens to Thomas the Doubter. He wants to touch Jesus – and this is granted – but Jesus says that touching is not what it's all about. 'Blessed are those who have not seen and yet have come to believe' (John 20.29). In other words, better to let go and believe. 'Why do you want the security of my presence?'

But then there is that wonderful moment at the beginning of the Acts of the Apostles where Jesus is taken from the disciples into heaven. They get a sharp kick in the pants from two men in white who've suddenly arrived on the scene. 'Men of Galilee, why do you stand looking up to heaven …?'

In other words, why are you clinging on to him, let him go, live without the physical presence, get on with the job.

And then, just to complete the argument, when the writer of the letter to the Ephesians talks about the ascension he gives it the most extended theological reflection on that moment in the New Testament. But in that reflection he does not dwell upon the actual incident itself, but talks about it as the source of mature life for the Church. He says it is the point at which Christ gives gifts to his people and fills all things. 'When he ascended on high . . . he gave gifts to his people.' 'He ascended far above all the heavens so that he might fill all things …' (Ephesians 4.8, 10).

So the New Testament accounts of the ascension do not dwell upon the question of movement, the movement is a metaphor for something else. The movement upwards is a metaphor for a form of abandonment, a signal for a sort of relinquishment into God with the recognition that once this relinquishment is made, then mysteriously everything is given back to you, and indeed far more than you had believed would be possible. Acceptance of the absence of Christ leads to a realization that all things are full of God. This is what is being described in the New Testament by means of the accounts of Jesus' ascension. It is not a physical movement, but an interior dynamic whereby those who follow Jesus are asked to live in relinquishment, abandoning all they want, or all they possess. This is so that instead of having some particular things, they may be given all things; and by entering into the absence of God they may find themselves in his fullness.

There is a great deal more in the Scriptures and in the Christian tradition about this absence or emptiness than we realize. It is hidden from us by our insistence upon fulfilment and the contemporary belief that fulfilment and completion of various kinds are possible and are our right. Living with absence and emptiness is regarded by many in society, especially by the popular magazine culture, as a form of disease, or at least something which can be put right. So long as you have the money!

But even a glance at the teaching of Jesus shows that this is not what he is saying. Jesus' insistence is on a readiness to live with that absence or emptiness so that we can be open to what we are not. Simon Tugwell comments on the Sermon on the Mount, saying 'All our jockeying for position, striving to get ourselves into a powerful and influential place, is the bluster which comes from a relative emptiness …' – or, I would add, the bluster which comes from an inability to accept emptiness and absence. He continues: 'We must learn to be incomplete, a space within which God can act …'[1] So the central teaching of Jesus is about the need for a self-emptying, what I would call an ascension, so that we can be filled with the creative word of God.

It is for all these reasons that Christians have to be enormously careful about what is called 'spiritual experience'. Much of what passes for spiritual experience in the contemporary Church risks being the spiritual equivalent of Mary Magdalene's clinging on to the Lord, a form of inability to relinquish yourself into God, a form of refusal of the ascension into the absence of God. There was a phase in Christian thinking when the Church looked back to the mystics with rose-coloured spectacles because, it was said, here was evidence of the centrality of experience of God in the life of the Church. It was felt that at least there had been something which points the way, and maybe we can find it again in our own barren age. But the evidence is that 'experience' of this kind is *not* what the mystics were talking about. What they were saying was that you have to relinquish these so-called spiritual states if you would be full of God. Indeed Meister Eckhart, the great German mystic who spent a great deal of his time as teacher of, and spiritual adviser to, the rather overheated communities of women under his care, says, 'Then how should I love God? You should love God unspiritually, that is your soul should be unspiritual and stripped of all spirituality, for so long as your soul has a spirit's form, it has images, and so long as it has images it has a medium, and so long as it has a medium it is not unity or simplicity.'[2] And a little further on he says – and this sums up so much of what I am trying to say – 'whoever is seeking God by ways is finding ways and losing God, who in ways is hidden'.

But you will shake your heads and resist this as far too radical. How can we be stripped of spirituality? Is this really what the ascension of Christ means? How did we get there from a headmaster's wife in north London?

Let me illustrate in musical terms. Those of you who worship in cathedrals regularly might know something of developments in the last hundred years in church music which are associated with the names of Langlais, Poulenc and Stravinsky. They composed some of the most terrifying settings of the mass. The effect of this music is electric. In one sense it is a great experience, but at another deeper level it is not an experience at all for such music leaves you empty, stripped out, not full of warmth or a sense of majesty, as you are, say, after listening to Stanford or Howells. After Langlais' *Messe Solennelle* you are scrubbed clean, as Eckhart says, 'without images'. And it is then at that point, when you are emptied, have relinquished all things, that you are, literally, full of joy. At that point all things resound with God. You have become a space within which God can act. Ideally that is what the whole liturgy should do – not fill you with churchy, spiritual feelings, but empty you, draw you into the reality of God so that you are then all joy, all unity, all simplicity. So that you are then ascended and ready to be Christ for all things and to find Christ in all things.

Say Hello to the Lady

'Blessed are those who have not seen and yet have come to believe' (John 20.29)

Those of you who are accustomed to taking your holidays in France might be surprised to know that Mary Magdalene got there before you. As you drive down the Autoroute du Sud, chasing the sun, you will pass the beautiful pilgrim church at Vézelay where her relics are reputedly held. And if you do get as far as Provence you will find that she was there as well, for the legend is that she, along with Mary the wife of Cleopas and Mary the wife of Zebedee, mother of James and John, and a number of others, fled from persecution in Jerusalem and landed in Provence at a place now known as Les Saintes Maries de la Mer. Mary Magdalene became a vigorous preacher in the south of France before her death and the transfer of her relics to Vézelay. But before you reject all this as the product of overheated medieval imagination of no use to us moderns, and think we should return to the facts as they are to be found in the Gospels, then pause for a while because it is not at all clear from the Gospel accounts as to what is fact and what is the product of theological imagination even there.

Much has been made of Mary Magdalene being the first to the tomb on that morning and the first to meet the risen Lord. Thus it is a woman to whom the risen Christ appears first and who announces this to the other disciples. She is celebrated as 'Apostola Apostolorum', apostle to the apostles. And all this has been, and continues to be, of much encouragement to the women in the Church, and rightly so.

But was this the intention of the author of the Gospel? He

certainly does not see her as the prime example of belief in the resurrection. That privilege he reserves for the Beloved Disciple who came to the tomb and 'saw and believed'. Mary is much more on a par with Thomas, who wanted to see and touch and was rebuked by Jesus, for 'Blessed are those who have not seen and yet have come to believe.' So Mary's clinging to Jesus is not right. 'Do not cling to me' is a reproach, in line with the reproach to Thomas, meaning 'You should not need to cling to me.'

It is because it is seen by the Gospel writer in that light that we cannot be totally sure of when it occurred. He has placed the appearance to Mary here so that it stands in contrast to the ready acceptance of 'sightless' faith by the Beloved Disciple, and in parallel with Thomas doubting. It therefore is positioned to make a point, and we know that this author is only too ready to move incidents around so that they fit his theological intentions. So the appearance to Mary could have been then or later, we simply don't really know.

The point I am making is that John's imagination has already been at work in the telling of the story of Mary Magdalene. He wants to portray her as someone who has to learn true discipleship, who – like Thomas – has to learn not to cling. So he writes the story accordingly. The consequence is that if you find yourself reacting against the medieval legends about Mary Magdalene as you drive through France on your holidays and want to find a sure historical point in the Gospel narratives and say, 'Ah, that's what really happened, I can be sure of that', then you will be deceived, because the Gospels themselves are part of that process of imaginative interpretation which we call the Christian tradition. You cannot easily reach beyond the process of imaginative interpretation to a sure point in the Gospels. Everything we have, right from the beginning, is coloured by, produced by, the imagination of faithful people.

Now before you throw your hands up in horror or despair, and say you thought that at least Christianity was a historical religion and ask, 'What is there to rely on now?', think for a while. In actual fact the modern stress on Christianity as a historical religion, and upon Christ as a particular historical figure, gives the Church and the believer more problems than it can cope with and distorts our discipleship. I have no wish whatsoever to deny that Christ was a man in history, but it would be far, far better to say that Christianity is an imaginative tradition – a stream of the imagination – than for us to say that it is historical, as if that was all that was needed. I believe that if we said that the Christian tradition was a stream of the imagination with a historical origin, then we would be far more 'evangelical' and we would find ourselves flooded with enquiries from modern people whose imaginations have been starved by a modernist Church – certainly more flooded than we are now, banging on as we do about facts and history and truth in the most unimaginative way.

You see, what has happened over the last hundred or more years is that we have abandoned imagination and have concentrated on the scientific historical study of the Gospel records. A vast industry of scholars has done remarkable work in discovering what can really be said about Jesus of Nazareth and his disciples. That's all well and good, but the more Jesus' life becomes part of history, the more he becomes particularized as a *man*, then the harder it becomes for all sorts of men and women to identify with him. You can see this happening in contemporary theology. Some women theologians are beginning to ask, 'Can a male Christ save women?' Indeed, this was a live discussion among the Catholic nuns that I once worked with. The homosexual community is asking whether or not Jesus shared their orientation. Such questions are really false ones and derive from a false historicism. It would be far better if Christ's maleness was not emphasized so much, and this maleness was not given the impossible burden of representing every range of human experience and problem in itself.

Another development in the modern Church has made the situation worse. There has been a decline in the popular understanding of the communion of saints. Once you jettison that element of Christian devotion, or say that it is all a product of tradition and outdated, or all a product of medieval monks inventing relics to get money out of tourists, then you have to focus exclusively upon Jesus as a role model for devotion. Once again, impossible burdens are placed upon him.

For St Paul Christ is the first of a body of people, the body being made up of all those who follow in his way and so are incorporated into his life, death and resurrection. He is the first of a body of examples. For most of Christian history Christ carried within himself a universal humanity, and drew all men and women into the divinity of God. Once you drop that universal humanity of Christ in favour of *a* historical particularity, then you make the communion of saints an impossibility.

The communion of saints, such a real feature of the Middle Ages, made it possible for everybody to be at home. It made it possible to see what sanctity might look like whoever you were and however different to Christ you might be. It made it possible for the married, the single, the female, the rich, the poor, the gay, the straight, the criminals, the different to see that there might be a way to God for them. Mary Magdalene was revered as the reformed prostitute. This was not anti-women or anti-sex, but showed that all could reach God, whoever they were. It made it possible for every kind of human being, of whatever strangeness, of whatever orientation, of whatever failing or success, to see that who they were could be included in God. If you didn't live in Palestine or weren't among the earliest apostles, then the distance could still be overcome.

This is why Christian devotion has Mary Magdalene come to France, and Joseph of Arimathea, thank God, to Glastonbury – to show French people and Somerset people that sanctity is within their grasp.

Christians are not those who stand on the towers of historical scholarship looking backwards into history with telescopes or special listening devices trying to find out from the past how to live now. They are those who stand together in their own times, holding hands with each other and holding hands with Mary Magdalene the penitent, with Joseph of Arimathea, with Andrew, with Mary, with Dunstan, with Martin Luther King, with Bonhoeffer and all the rest, in order to live lives like Christ's now as he holds hands with us all.

So, as you drive down to Provence, stop off at Vézelay and say hello to the lady. Or, if you get as far as Florence, go into the baptistery of the cathedral and see her there, carved in wood by Donatello, a gaunt and haggard penitent, symbol, friend of all of us who would come to Christ, whoever we are and whatever our past may have been.

When you see her you will know that the friendship of God is infinite.

Notes

Introduction

1   Julian of Norwich, *Showings (Long Text)*, eds Edmund Colledge
    and James Walsh, Classics of Western Spirituality, New York:
    Paulist Press, 1978.
2   Thomas Traherne, *Centuries of Meditations*, ed. Bertram Dobell,
    London: P. J. and A. E. Dobell, 1927.
3   John Milbank, Catherine Pickstock and Graham Ward (eds),
    Radical Orthodoxy, London: Routledge, 1999.
4   H. A. Williams, *The True Wilderness*, London: Constable, 1965,
    p. 8ff.

2   The Long Lunch

1   Alice Walker, *The Color Purple*, London: The Women's Press,
    1983, pp. 165 and 167.

3   The English Patient

1   Thomas Traherne, *Centuries of Meditations*, ed. Bertram Dobell,
    London: P. J. and A. E. Dobell, 1927, p. 24.
2   Teresa of Avila, *The Interior Castle* 5.1.11, trans. Kieran Kavanaugh
    and Otilo Rodriguez, Classics of Western Spirituality, New York:
    Paulist Press, 1979, p. 90.

4   How Many Muscles in the Head of a Caterpillar?

1   Sara Maitland, *A Big-Enough God: Artful Theology*, London:
    Mowbray, 1994, p. 103.

5 Are We Erotic Enough?

1 Origen, *Commentary on the Song of Songs*, cited by Bernard McGinn, *The Foundations of Mysticism*, Vol. 1, London: SCM Press, 1991, p. 118.
2 Song of Solomon 2.10–11, 16; 1.2 (AV).
3 Julian of Norwich, *Showings (Long Text)*, eds Edmund Colledge and James Walsh, Classics of Western Spirituality, New York: Paulist Press, 1978, p. 231.
4 Paul Tillich, *Love, Power and Justice*, New York and London: Oxford University Press, 1954, p. 30.

6 How Far Does Your Personality Go?

1 Iris Murdoch, *The Time of the Angels*, London: Chatto & Windus, 1966.
2 David S. Cunningham, *These Three Are One*, Oxford: Blackwell, 1998.

7 'Music Heard So Deeply…'

1 Vikram Seth, *An Equal Music*, London: Phoenix, 1999.
2 Thomas Merton, *Conjectures of a Guilty Bystander*, 2nd edition, London: Sheldon Press, 1977, p. 217.
3 T. S. Eliot, 'The Dry Salvages', *Four Quartets*, London: Faber, 1943.

8 'You Must Change Your Life'

1 Rainer Maria Rilke, 'Archaic Torso of Apollo', in *New Poems*, trans. Stephen Cohn, Manchester: Carcanet Press Ltd, 1997.
2 Song of Solomon 2.10–11.

9 Teaching a Stone to Talk

1 Annie Dillard, *Teaching a Stone to Talk: Expeditions and Encounters*, New York: Harper & Row, 1983, paperback 1988, p. 67.
2 Exodus 20.18.

3   John Milbank, Catherine Pickstock and Graham Ward (eds),
    Radical Orthodoxy, London: Routledge, 1999.
4   *The Apostolic Tradition*, cited by Olivier Clément, *The Roots of
    Christian Mysticism*, London: New City, 1993, p. 193.
5   Ann and Barry Ulanov, *Primary Speech*, London: SCM Press,
    1985, p. ix.
6   Seamus Heaney, *The Government of the Tongue*, London: Faber,
    1988, p. 107.

12 'I Think You Should Unravel Yourself...'

1   Seamus Heaney, *The Government of the Tongue*, London: Faber,
    1988, pp. 107–8.

13 'More Pieces Than I Began with ...'

1   Henri Nouwen, *Reaching Out*, London: Collins, 1976, p. 30.

14 Eating with Defiled Hands

1   Miroslav Wolf, *Exclusion and Embrace*, Nashville, TN: Abingdon
    Press, 1996.

15 In Praise of Hildegard of Bingen – Obit 17 September 1179

1   Hildegard of Bingen, *Book of Divine Works*, cited by Grace Jantzen,
    Power, Gender and Christian Mysticism, Cambridge: Cambridge
    University Press, 1995, p. 228.

16 Julian of Norwich

1   Julian of Norwich, *Showings (Long Text)*, eds Edmund Colledge
    and James Walsh, Classics of Western Spirituality, New York:
    Paulist Press, 1978.
2   René Girard, in James G. Williams (ed.), *The Girard Reader*, New
    York: Crossroad, 1996.

17 The 1940s House

1 Isaiah 43.2.

18 Things Fall Apart

1 Kathleen Norris, *Amazing Grace*, New York: Riverhead Books, 1998, paperback edition Oxford: Lion Publishing, 2000.
2 William Shakespeare, *King Lear*, Act 5, Scene 3.

20 The Passion of Our Lord Jesus Christ According to St Mark

1 Since writing this section I have read John Fenton's book *More About Mark* (SPCK, 2001) and have been very struck by the many parallels between what he says and my own approach. I am grateful to Canon Charles Shells for bringing this book to my attention.
2 Kathleen Raine, *The Inner Journey of the Poet*, London: Allen & Unwin, 1982.
3 Charles Causley, 'I am the Great Sun', *Collected Poems 1951–2000*, Basingstoke: Macmillan, 2000.
4 Francis Thompson, *The Hound of Heaven*, London and Oxford: Mowbray, 1947.
5 R. S. Thomas, *Counterpoint*, Newcastle upon Tyne: Bloodaxe Books, 1990, p. 54.

21 The Anointing of Jesus

1 Tina Beattie, *The Last Supper According to Martha and Mary*, London: Continuum Press, 2001.
2 Song of Solomon 8.6–7.

22 Ascension as Absence

1 Simon Tugwell, *Reflection on the Beatitudes*, London: Darton, Longman & Todd, 1980, pp. 48ff.
2 Meister Eckhart, Sermon 5b, *The Essential Sermons*, eds Edmund Colledge and Bernard McGinn, London: SPCK, p. 183.